A
Sourcebook
of Christmas
Meditations

The Heart Has Its Seasons

Wheaton Phillips Webb

LUX CHRISTI

ABINGDON PRESS • NASHVILLE

THE HEART HAS ITS SEASONS:

A Sourcebook of Christmas Meditations

Copyright © 1982 by Abingdon

Second Printing 1983

Library of Congress Cataloging in Publication Data

WEBB, WHEATON PHILLIPS, 1911–
  The heart has its seasons.
  1. Christmas—Meditations. I. Title.
  BV45.W35   242'.33   82-3898   AACR2

ISBN 0-678-16800-7 (pbk.)

MANUFACTURED BY THE PARTHENON PRESS AT
NASHVILLE, TENNESSEE, UNITED STATES OF AMERCA

For Alice
and a parsonage
in a pear tree
♡

Contents

The Heart Has Its Seasons

The heart has its seasons—
Christmas is one of them
a time for remembering,
and glad tidings of great joy.

The light diminishes all these thronged December days,
but in our rush to hold onto the light
The Giver of Light will understand.

We press into his hands
the gifts whose costs
we do not stop to count—
love and our dreams
and memories of nights the stars came out.

The gifts he seeks
are never for himself,
but for his children
who reach out to us.

Noel!

Train Round the Bend

In the first gray gleams of early morning light I am listening for the train. It is coming round the bend now, tooting its whistle four times for every crossing as if it had been entrusted with waking up the town.

It has this in common with Christmas. The four Sundays of Advent are like the engineer's whistle, occasions with candles and carols to wake us up to the wonder of Christmas.

Christmas gifts, the ones that are sure to be cherished, are not hard to find—a book of verse if you are young and in love; maybe a shoehorn with a long handle for someone who finds it hard to stoop; mittens you knitted with your own arthritic hands for the hands of a child.

I pray a trinity of gifts for all those I love this Christmastide—three friends to sing a carol, three stars in the sky to light you through the winter, and the Three who are ever One to be to you and yours comfort and strength through all your days. So Christmas steals upon us with a peal of bells and the eyes of children all stars and dreams.

It sends up its old, old signals, a wreath upon your door and the fragrance of cookies baking in all the ovens down your street.

I can hear the last low wail of the whistle as the train leaves the valley to its silences. Like the train, Advent's four Sundays will come and go, but leave the best of all gifts, a silence full of mystery in the waiting heart.

On Getting Confused by Christmas

You say it is only the first week into Advent, and already you are so confused you do not know where to turn? Take heart. If you lived in Prague where the Czech Communists have a pathological hostility to Christmas, you would be climbing the wall. Here, for example, is an edict from the government.

> Because Christmas Eve falls on a Thursday, the day has been designated a Saturday for work purposes. Factories will close all day, with stores open a half day only. Friday, December 25, has been designated a Sunday, with both factories and stores open all day. Monday, December 28, will be a Wednesday for work purposes. Wednesday, December 30, will be a business Friday. Saturday, January 2, will be a Sunday, and Sunday, January 3, will be a Monday.

You can see that Christmas has the Communists completely unhinged. What was supposed to bring in the thousand years of peace has instead befuddled the imagination, confused the calendar, scuttled "Silent Night," and given the population the screaming meemies.

I don't know what I can do to get the Communists out of their Christmas confusion. Maybe I will go to Prague and sing "Good King Wenceslaus," which is a carol about the king the Czechs loved best. He died about A.D. 929—(or was it maybe 935?) things were confused in those days too.

You remember how the good saint looked out on the Feast of Stephen and saw a poor man gathering winter fuel, and how he set out with his page to bring the poor man a good dinner, only the page quickly lost heart because of the biting cold of the winter's night. But saints like Wenceslaus leave heat in the very sod they tread on, and the page walked home warm in the footprints of good King Wenceslaus.

As I will tell the story to the Communists, they will forget the confusion of turning Thursday into Sunday, and Christmas will arrive on time. I will tell them how Christianity came to the Czechs in the Middle Ages about a century before King Wenceslaus when Louis the Fat baptized fourteen Bohemian lords on January 13, 845, and started Christianity on its way in his land.

In spite of the Communists thinking they are up-to-date, you can see they are confused when it comes to Christmas. But good King Wenceslaus could have told them, and so could Louis the Fat, that here is one day of the year you chaps need not fool around with because it belongs to One everyone-in-the-know has been looking for ever since.

The Donkey as Presiding Genius

Christmas is often a boisterous season. Icy winds wander down chimneys. Poor shepherds are chilled to the bone. Some of the friendly beasts in the crèche on the church lawn blow away. So it was one memorable Yuletide. As I was passing by, a sudden gust lifted the lamb out of his miniature Bethlehem and tumbled him into the street.

I made a flying tackle, rescued the lamb, and installed him safely beside the door of my study inside the church. A patient little creature, he was surely a fitting symbol for a pastor (which is the beautiful old Latin word for "shepherd"), one who is known at times to engage in woolgathering.

My family tells me that I am not very observant, and I fear this is true. It was only after the lamb had been stationed at my door for several days that someone took the trouble to point out that it was not a lamb; It was a donkey with a donkey's long and ridiculous ears. People passing my door began to put their head in to look at me as if they wondered why their pastor found a donkey such a suitable symbol for his profession.

Nevertheless, I became a stout defender of donkeys, creatures our Lord must have loved, since he chose one for his last journey to Jerusalem, and everyone remembered the prophecy that when Messiah came he would not be mounted on a war horse but oh a humble beast.

"There is no glory in outstripping donkeys," the old epigrammatist Martial used to say, but one would like to keep Christmas remembering that donkeys sometimes discern the shining things your Philistine is bound to miss. I seem to remember a donkey who saw an angel before his master did (Numbers 22:21-35). The humble little beast was alert to the presence of the Most High before wiser heads were aware.

How wonderful if it were obligatory for a donkey to be installed just outside the door of the White House! Whoever happened to be president would take notice every day and remember that the little creature had seen angels of mercy before any heads of state had detected them. The President would think about the angels the donkey had seen and how angels like to sing about peace on earth. The president would fall flat on his face the way Balaam did; and he would say to God, "I did not know that you stood in the road confronting me" (NEB).

Yuletidily Yours

The fire is dying away to an ember on the hearth, and Beth is doing handsprings that end in a handstand with both her feet planted in the North Sea. On the map of England hanging on the wall of our family room, the North Sea is a pretty blue.

Upside down, Beth is just tall enough for her toes to touch the Isle of Lindisfarne where St. Cuthbert lived in the Middle Ages. St. Cuthbert used to plunge into the North Sea's icy waters and stand all day as a discipline. Whatever it was in himself that he was disciplining, it seems like an awful way to get rid of it.

"Beth, come down off that wall! You can't spend your whole life in the North Sea. You'll catch your death—and Christmas is coming."

Presently, while Alice and I are thumbing through the catalogues, we reach one of those perennial indecisions as to the merits of various toys for the seven grandsons. Here, for example, is a remarkable new gun that shoots blasts of air at a picture of a ferocious gorilla and slices it to ribbons. I argue vigorously for this wonder, with hopes of trying it out myself before it is wrapped in a Christmas package. But Alice, who is the embodiment of wisdom, sees a wrinkle in pingpong games that is more likely to taper off the energies of the small fry—and she wins out against the blowgun.

It is extraordinary how a woman can argue so cogently and never drop a stitch. She is knitting woolly mysteries in which to wrap beguiling granddaughters and is observing how truly remarkable grandchildren seem to be these days.

The evening is drawing to a close, and it is time to let St. Luke have the last word. His Bethlehem story is so beautiful that Beth has come down off the wall and stopped dipping into the North Sea. Even the fire leaps up happily as if to celebrate the one story that always comes out right.

Outside, the falling snow is performing its ancient redemption of the earth. When we wake to a white Christmas we shall turn again to a favorite of ours, an old Celtic poem, "The Blessing of the Kindling."

I will kindle my fire this morning
In the presence of the holy angels of heaven,
In the presence of Ariel of the loveliest forms,
In the presence of Uriel of the myriad charms,
Without malice, without jealousy, without envy,
Without fear, without terror of anyone under the sun,
But the Holy Son of God to shield me.

God, kindle thou in my heart within
A flame of love to my neighbor,
To my foe, to my friend, to my kindred all,
To the brave, to the knave, to the thrall,
O Son of the loveliest Mary,
From the lowliest thing that liveth,
To the Name that is highest of all.

And a Peace-Pillow Christmas for You

If you know our house at all, you know that we have had
candle Christmases when we made handsome tapers and got
covered with wax, and egg Christmases when Alice mounted
golden angels inside eggs and decorated the tree with them,
and cooky Christmases when all the cookies turned into stars
and gingerbread men. One year we had a cardinal Christmas
when Alice made the most stunning redbirds you ever saw and
flew them onto the Christmas tree. One Christmas we had as
our centerpiece a Santa Claus sleigh made out of a turkey
breastbone, and very convincing too!

This year we are planning a peace-pillow Christmas to
celebrate the old-fashioned peace in the heart. Maybe you
would like to make a peace pillow too. It does not have to be

larger than the slim balsam pillows your grandmother loved. Stuff it with the dried herbs you like best, lavender and rosemary and marjoram. Then, when the world is too much with you, lie down and cover your eyes with your peace pillow. Breathe deep of its fragrances. The first thing you know you are drowsy. Then wake to discover that the God of all peace is the strength of your days.

Mrs. Biebesheimer
and the Four Thousand Turkeys

The fire on our hearth is purring like a contented cat, and Alice is popping corn in the big old aluminum kettle that always works wonders. A December wind is busy at the decorations on our door, and Christmas is coming.

It is a time to feel rueful about all desolate things—little firs that are not given a second look when you are scouting for a Christmas tree; lambs that shiver in cold byres; and children wide-eyed with their first knowledge of what a world without love might turn out to be.

Here at our hearth we are doing some high remembering—for instance, of the time when the four boys were little and how one day they kicked a football—oh, a very bad punt—across the living room and smashed the two delicate Danish figurines on the mantle, and how no one was spanked, and besides, if you are rearing boys, it is nonsense to display china figurines, and anybody with sense will replace them with a bronze buffalo.

We are thinking too of Beth's Sunday school teacher, Mrs. Biebesheimer. Only Beth could never remember her name until one Christmas we visited a farm where four thousand turkeys all rushed upon us screaming, "Biebesheimer! Biebesheimer! Biebesheimer!" which is what four thousand turkeys really scream when they think you are going to give them some corn. From that hour Beth remembered her Sunday school teacher's name—learned it from the turkeys.

But now the fire on our hearth is making little flickerings to attract our attention as if it wished it could have some of Alice's inspired popcorn or could be human and chat with us awhile.

As Christmas comes, I can't think of anything better than the love that is forever mixing itself up with starlight and candles and mistletoe and shepherds and other men (not always wise), and with bells in all the steeples pealing out the glory that the Christ we love is born.

The Second-Best Angel

I wish that everyone I love could visit our Christmas tree and sit awhile and have a cup of kindness. You always find two angels on our tree, a splendid one at the top who lords it over all and another precariously balanced on a lower branch. This one is made of golden straw, but if the straws keep breaking off from her skirt, in a few years she will be the world's first mini-skirted angel.

Nevertheless, as far as I can see, she is just as proud as her sister at the top of the tree. Really, we like the second-best angel better. She may be a little the worse for wear, but she looks on the straw Child in her arms just as if she were the superior angel at the top.

O second-best angel, live forever! You may never rise to the highest echelon of the heavenly host. You may have to remain with lower choirs instead of soaring to the ranks of the seraphim. But there is a place for you. You in your tattered skirt are a gentle reminder of the ghosts of Christmas past and of the days when there were four small boys and later a very satisfying daughter around the tree on Christmas morning.

And now, second-best angel, after all you have endured from the hands of children, you display no envy because another angel reigns at the top of the tree. Maybe it is because you have been holding the Child lovingly in your arms all these years. Because you have kept your eyes on him, your rank on the Christmas tree is of little concern to you.

You, O second-best angel, will understand the meaning of the occasion late in the life of St. Thomas Aquinas, when he laid his pen aside for the last time, leaving his *Summa* unfinished because, as he said, "I have seen that which makes all that I have written look like straw."

Ah! That is not very polite of him, O second-best angel, because you are made of straw. But because you are still cradling the Child in your arms, you will be the last to hold a grudge.

Thou Child of All Our Waiting Hearts

It was one of those afternoons in late November when gray light filters through old church windows where the spider has wrought his webs and induces its own special kind of gloom. In an empty church silences crowd the heart. This, you tell yourself, is the way medieval monks must have felt the stillness of ancient abbies.

I shall never know what induced me to unlock the door and climb the stairs to the dim loft behind our altar. The loft is a place of shadows to shake the heart when you enter it alone in the cheerless dusk. A wintry light fell bleakly through its single window.

Of course it was absurd to think that anyone could be there. But then, I saw them, their faces rapt, their eyes unblinking, as if they had been bowing for long ages in reverence, the all but life-size figures of our Christmas crèche. They huddled in the cold, unstirring, peering into the gloom as if they knew that only a very special starlight could penetrate such darkness as now hovered over them.

"Mary!" I said softly. "Joseph!" And then, "Thou Child of all our waiting hearts!" And I felt a sudden impulse to embrace the donkey who never feels that Christmas will come again until we invite him and all other gentle beasts to join us at the manger on the church lawn.

Slowly I withdrew from the Holy Family as one might from a throne where one has come to pay homage to a king. At first, I did not want to pray, only to remember. I remembered how I used to visit the barn of a neighboring shepherd with my four small sons on Christmas Eve. We sat in a mow of sweet-smelling hay with the sheep nearby and became shepherds and wise men and pretended that we were lucky enough to have been in Bethlehem the night the great star shone.

Then I remembered a child who whispered to her mother when she saw the wise men descending the aisle of our village church, "I know that God is coming through the door, —but I don't know which one he is."

And I remembered this from the letter of a friend: "I long for a Christmas where no one gives anyone anything except love, but I suppose even then, human nature being what it is, there would be a few exchanges the day after."

Maybe not. If one were to commune, not just at Advent, but for a twelvemonth with the Holy Family in its modest loft above

17

the altar. Or if one could hear the choirs of great churches echoing the *Gloria in excelsis Deo* that once was sung above that other manger. Or if one can still reach out in his spirit to touch all those he loves in a thousand homes nestled under friendly chimneys.

Of Christmas Ghosts and Other Haunts

If you have ever sat around a hearth on a December evening with the snow tapping at your window like a ghostly hand and the wind worrying the fire, you can imagine us at the parsonage now. The big problem is always apples or popcorn. You reach for another handful of corn and decide that you would like to live through eternity with the taste of popcorn on your tongue. Then you select another juicy red Jonathan and decide it's apples you'll live with forever.

At the moment I am sitting on the old green hassock by the fire with Beth on my knee and doing my best to terrify my captive audience with a gothic ballad I wrote long ago about the Leeds ghost. The most bloodcurdling stanza of this thriller rises to great heights.

> And some have seen upon the rocks
> A wild disheveled singer
> With a lighted taper burning bright
> Upon each bloodless finger.

Even Herbert seems to shudder. She is the only one-eyed girl doll named Herbert in the universe as far as we know. Beth, who has had more than enough of my gothic ballad, is about to move over to her mother's lap. Alice, who is rocking in the Boston rocker, has the look in her eye of a woman who wonders whether she dares try out on company one of the astonishing recipes she has just clipped from her favorite magazine.

If the wind wafts over to your house some of the heavenly fragrance of our popcorn, or any whisper of the derring-do of our Christmas ghost, take it as a sign that Alice has just put her whistling teakettle on the stove and is waiting for a knock on the door.

Christmas Is a Candle

Alice and I and Beth—her eyes wide in wonder—are sitting here in the lovely silence of the church in the December dusk remembering. How still a sanctuary can be when winter snow is falling!

Beth whispers a question about the Advent wreath in the chancel. Its handsome circle of evergreens surrounds four tall candles, one to be lighted each of the succeeding Sundays of Advent. The candles, we explain to the child, symbolize the Light that has come into the world with Christ.

It is a good time to be still and to remember

> . . . the faces of a thousand friends we love whose kindness is a lamp of purest gold
> . . . the faces of kith and kin, some living far away, who seem, when we pray for them, to be as near as the beating of our hearts

. . . the carols that bring all heaven raining down in silver melody

. . . and the vision Christmas always brings of a "Holy Family" trooping down the aisle in Christmas pageants to disappear again into the ultimate mystery, so that you know that Christ may be born of you too.

All these things we are thinking of, and if wishes were angels, you would see at your window even now a visitor from the cloven sky and hear again the ancient *Gloria*.

Beth is asking if she may light one of the candles in the Advent wreath. As it begins to burn, our love goes forth to covet for you a Christmas Eve with a great star shining low in the sky above your door.

Come, Christmas, Come!

"Jump, Jip, jump!"

Beth, who is six, has brought her reader home from school. She is regaling the family with the adventures of Alice and Jerry, two characters in her reader, and their faithful dog Jip. Alice and Jerry seldom venture beyond words of one syllable or sentences of more than three words. This is having a deteriorating effect on my prose style, since we have all fallen into the habit of talking like the people in Beth's book.

"Come, Alice, come!"

—another line from the famous reader—and Alice comes.

All three of us are sitting on this December evening in the warm lamplight on the green davenport opposite the fire. Beth continues with the story, which she is either reading very well or repeating by rote.

> "See the squirrel.
> Look up, Alice,
> See the squirrel."

It is all very beguiling, this miracle of learning to read, and we are properly impressed. The fire is whispering secrets on the hearth, and the wind is whimpering sad little sounds in the chimney as if it were eager to be invited in for popcorn. The mountain of popcorn in its lordly bowl is disappearing as Beth gets deeper into the story. At this point Jerry sees three squirrels, and Jip is after them.

> "Jump, Jip, jump!"

The flame of our Christmas candle is flickering mysteriously, and I can see that it is flirting with the wind in the chimney. Beth is about to finish the story of Alice and Jerry and Jip. She is yawning as if she realizes that her prose style is being ruined too.

> "I see it, Jerry.
> It is something little.
> It can play with you.
> It can play with me.
> It is my little puppy."

"Come, Beth, come," Alice is saying, and Beth, with the resistance children always muster to deal with the suggestion that they retire, is concocting a delaying action.

At last I am alone looking lazily at the fire, wondering if there are. sermons in it or dreams or memories or promises-for-keeps. The clock is ticking away eternity, and the house drowses in the warm possession of sleep.

I will climb the stairs and look on the face of the sleeping child. Once there was that other Child who dreamed of shepherds and angels and the old and wise ones coming to his birth. That was very long ago, but it is not hard to find our way back to the place of his lowly birth in a season that holds its choicest gifts in store for you, gifts of love and goodwill.

"Come, Christ, come!"

Through a Keyhole in the Parsonage Door

Four nights till Christmas, and the parsonage is far from still as a mouse. At the moment we are enjoying the dancing flames on the hearth, sampling Alice's famous fruitcake, and making Christmas plans. The wind howling down the chimney reminds me of the one-room country schoolhouse where I learned "The Wreck of the *Hesperus*." I am reciting it now, with one arm around Beth, sitting beside me on a big green hassock watching the fire.

> Come hither, come hither! my little daughter,
>   And do not tremble so;
> For I can weather the roughest gale
>   That ever the wind did blow.

Beth clutches her three dolls, Herbert, Patience, and Pizzle-um Siv—that is how some people pronounce Psalm CIV—and says, "I love you forty-six." Forty-six means "very much." She picked it up from her big brother, who mutters his mathematics aloud sometimes when he is puzzled. Beth follows him around, all six feet of him, when he is home.

Alice has just dropped a stitch in the mittens she is knitting for the church's mitten tree while the *Hesperus* is foundering off Norman's Woe. But at last the mitten is finished. The poor *Hesperus* is still afloat but is one solid sheet of ice and cannot last much longer. And Beth is nodding.

The plain truth is, if you hope to achieve a thumping, God-bless-us-everyone, Tiny-Tim kind of feeling, it is time to organize for it. Sit around a fire if you can find one. Soak up all the warmth and gaiety the heart can take. Say a prayer for "all huddled birds that thought that song was dead."

"So hallow'd and so gracious is the time."

The Day Santa Lost His Head

One of the best things ever to hit our town was the Santa Claus who used to occupy a corner in a drugstore window every December. He was a handsome figure in his red plush suit, purring away as he ceaselessly waggled his head. One blustery day I went sauntering past the store only to find that he was no longer there. A clerk told me sadly, "He was wagging his head one day when it fell off, and we—er—had to dispose of it."

I shed a tear. A Santa like that one doesn't come along more than once in a lifetime. Then I began to wonder about some of the things that would make Santa shake his head until it fell off.

Maybe he was shaking it in sadness for children who get showered with presents every Christmas, but not with genuine love the year around. Even a wonderful toy is no substitute for loving-kindness.

Maybe he could not forget the hunger in the midst of bounty that is possible in our land. Maybe he was remembering the

23

face of a hungry child surviving on the inadequate diet of the poor even as he was reading an advertisement for twelve platinum ornaments—only $5000—for the Christmas tree that has everything.

Maybe he was shaking his head because he knew we Americans are capable of so much downright kindness and good intention at the same time we have stockpiled enough atomic bombs to wipe out everybody in the world fifteen times.

Maybe Santa was hearing again that strange song from the sky, "Peace on earth, good will toward men," and was shaking his head because these ingredients were missing in so many places.

I hope that down at the corner drugstore things straighten out and that they find Santa's missing head and that all of us do some beautiful things to set his head wagging in approval.

On Opening a Door

"Doorstep Baby Abandoned Twice on Birthday"—this was a headline we read in the *Yorkshire Evening Post* when we were in the North Riding. On the day of its birth the mother of the child had put him in a cardboard box and covered him with a woolen sheet and a wool sweater. She attached a letter asking whoever found the little stranger to care for him.

Someone did find the child but left him again on the doorstep of a hospital with a second note that said, "Did not want to get involved."

You cannot help thinking about that abandoned baby and about that other Child who was left on the doorstep of the world. Parallels come to mind, but in the case of that other

Child the tender arms of Mary were waiting to embrace him, and her sweet voice to sing the *Magnificat* with its compassion for the disregarded.

As years passed, many who would find her Child would later leave him on the doorstep of the church with the feeling that they had done their duty and "did not want to get involved."

But there would always be others who knew about doorsteps and how cold they could be for a Child. They opened their doors. They found the Child and took him into their hearts. Now, because they had touched him, it was easier to get involved in all the loving ways the heart can know.

So I hope that whenever you hear the whisper of a footstep in the snow, you will open your door. As you embrace the one you find on your doorstep, you will never doubt that the Love that came down at Christmas has come knocking.

Crash! There Goes the Littlest Cherub

The littlest cherub was proud of his niche in the nativity scene in the window at the parsonage. For more Advents than I can remember he had been kneeling reverently at the foot of the Virgin. It was evident that he liked being there, sheltering a tiny candle in his folded hands.

But now he was beyond repair, head missing, wings shattered, a candidate for the broom and dustpan. A wingless victory, it was his duty to sing the praise of heaven, and being headless, this was hard.

I swept him up, poor fellow. He had really gone all to pieces, but it was then I thought I heard him speaking to me and to all the dear people at Old Friendly First.

"It is true," he was saying, "that, like me, none of you has wings yet. As far as I can see, you haven't even begun to sprout them. But if you were ever to deny the love the Lord puts in your hearts, it would be as bad as losing your wings.

"And, unlike me, all of you have heads. But if you were to stop using your imaginations in making the witness of your beautiful church even more effective, it would be as bad as losing your head entirely—like me."

"Poor chap!" I said to the littlest cherub, "I'm afraid that now that you're all broken up you have started preaching."

I could see that he would have nodded his head if he had had one. And I thought—you can hardly help shuddering, can you? How awful it would be for a church like ours to lose its head and its wings when the Lord Christ needs us whole.

And a Parsonage in a Pear Tree

The Advent stars are pouring down their glints of glory, and we are sitting around the hearth at the parsonage—Alice, Beth, and I. While no one is doing anything very remarkable, we are all doing it with abandon. Alice is braiding a rug that grows and grows, a project for a lifetime that turns last year's wools into this year's wonders, and all very colorful too.

Beth is looking for her shoes. She is almost always looking for her shoes. She is growing up to be a very satisfying daughter, but will probably always go on misplacing things, if her first ten years are any indication. Every day or two the whole family has a campaign to find her shoes. We guess it is her destiny to go through life barefoot.

Tillie, the no-account but greatly loved dog who was starving when she first came to us, is dreaming by the fire with an I-wish-I-had-a-bone look in her brown binking eyes. Dogs *do* communicate well.

To anyone who has not tried it I recommend this unremarkable way to spend an evening in Advent. If you turn your mind loose for a while, you will think of a thousand faces you love, and you will hear the lilt of old carols as young people come trooping to your door.

Beth has found her shoes—they were under a crib for a Barbie doll. Alice has run out of wool for her rug and is eyeing a perfectly good coat of mine in hopes of weaving it into her rug—not a chance! Tillie has gone to sleep, and from the way she thumps her tail and whines I presume she is on the trail of a squirrel.

Shhh! Speak softly, or you'll break the spell of a winter evening.

The Lion Lies Down with the Lamb

It was Christmas Eve, twelve of the clock. The parsonage was still except for the sound of something nuzzling up to the lamb in the crèche under the Christmas tree. It was Tillie, the greatly beloved, if no-account dog whose nose was quivering at the symbols of the Yuletide. At last her curiosity was satisfied, and she stretched herself beside the lamb and yawned.

This is exactly the way Isaiah promised it would be.

The wolf shall dwell with the lamb,
    and the leopard shall lie down with the kid,

and the calf and the lion and the fatling together,
and a little child shall lead them. (Isaiah 11:6)

There under our Christmas tree was the peaceable
kingdom. There, too, in the manger, where a fond Mary and
Joseph regarded him with rapt faces, was the little Child who is
to lead us into the realm of the great reconciliation. There are
so many of us to be reconciled to each other, and maybe, as
Marian Anderson once proposed, it will be through music that
we become able to grasp one another's souls.

If the Lord God can create, no doubt he can also reconcile
lions and wolves and lambs and leopards and kids and calves
and all the other varieties of us. He can do it because he has sent
a little Child to help us find the way into his peaceable
kingdom.

On Not Being Given a Dog for Christmas

Rejoice as you may in all the Christmas gifts you have
received, did it ever occur to you that the ones you cherish most
are the ones you were afraid you were going to receive but
didn't?

It happened somewhat so last Christmas at our house. Tillie,
the faithful family dog of many years, had died, and sorry as we
were to be without her, we had to admit that there was
something to be said for not having to return at a certain hour
to feed her. A beautiful sense of freedom we had forgotten
about descended on Wit's Other End, which is what we call the
parsonage.

Then, the night before Christmas, came an unsettling

long-distance call from a small boy who is as sharp as grandsons come. I could detect the too, too eager eagerness in his voice and felt an apprehension at what was coming.

"Don't tell," he said, "but you're going to get a dog for Christmas."

I saw my illusions of spending my last peaceful years without a pup, seeping away at the threat of a Christmas present that would wag its tail and bark at the mailman.

"You wouldn't—?" I said, feeling my face blanch.

"It's a beautiful dog. You'll love him," the boy insisted.

I do not know how you tell a grandson obsessed with giving you a dog that under no circumstances are you going to become attached to another dog.

Happily, my fears were groundless. The dog that this child was out to give me belonged to his whole neighborhood, and it had been trying to give it away for years.

Christmas dawned crisp and white without the burden of another pup to train—and no doubt fall for. It struck me then that, though most gifts that come our way at Christmas are a delight to us, there is great satisfaction in some of the gifts we did not receive. I asked myself if I had ever been properly grateful to the Creator for things the withholding of which has proved to be life's choicest blessing.

I thought of some of the things that I had once wanted very much and that, if they had come my way, would not have added any final splendor.

A trip to the Holy Land—this I used to think would be the greatest. Then I found that I could imagine a Holy Land, and my own private Holy Land is so much better than the one I never got to visit that there is no comparison.

Or I think of old books that once I wanted and never found, like Geoffrey of Monmouth's *History of Glastonbury Abbey,* which after a lifetime still eludes me, but which has become more valuable by the happy sense of adventure that still is mine whenever I cross the threshold of a secondhand bookstore.

Each of us will have his personal list of gifts he was glad not to receive, but which are so satisfactory in their failure to arrive. This Christmas be glad for small grandsons—and the dogs they do not give you.

Eight Maids A-milking, Ten Lords A-leaping

Before I realized what I was doing, I had done it.

There on my doorstep was one of the sure signs Christmas was coming, a plate of delicious cookies, but with nothing to identify the friendly cookie maker. I guessed a dozen people, good neighbors, old friends, who knew my weakness for Christmas cookies.

I popped a beautiful cookie enameled with red and white into my mouth. Alas, too late I discovered I had bitten the hand of Santa Claus. According to the news, a psychiatric research team has diagnosed my deed and says it is happening oftener than you would think this time of year.

> Christmas in the United States has become a breeder of mental depression and infantile behavior and a reminder of an unhappy past for some people. . . . It can be a headache for people who don't want to play the holiday game as it has developed in American culture.

I guess there must be people who would not hesitate to bite the hand of Santa Claus and who would refuse to give a hand to good King Wenceslaus when he is gathering winter fuel. Maybe when they were young they pricked their fingers on holly, and now they are against all hanging of the greens. If they have not moved around very much in the world of the Spirit, it is not surprising that they have a native suspicion of it and do not see that if they are ever to reclaim their lost festivities, they must take new heart.

Ah, but you lucky ones who have received the new heart: Suddenly life for you ceases to be humdrum and dusty. It's eight maids a-milking and ten lords a-leaping. It's great choirs raising the roof with their hallelujahs. It's Jeannette and Isabella bringing their torch to see the place where the young Child lies.

A new heart—that is what it takes. It you have it, you will feel a little rueful even at biting the hand of a Santa Claus cookie because the cookie is so beautiful. Thank you, Mrs. Anonymous, for leaving those delicious cookies at my door.

The Angels Were Flying Backward

The Advent supper at church was in full swing. The tables were brilliantly decorated with the symbols of Christmas as it is celebrated in many lands. At my table a happy little angel chime from Norway was spinning. Four small candles gave off rising heat, turning a louvered wheel to which the angels were attached. The golden angels were blowing tiny trumpets and kicking up their heels at bells as they merrily whirled around.

Almost at the same moment everyone at our table exclaimed, "The angels are flying backward!" They certainly were. Someone had made the mistake of assembling the louvered wheel upside down.

I guess that there is plenty these days that an angel would

want to back away from. When you think of what we promised God in our hearts at the end of the Second World War, and how we have repeatedly broken our promises in the generations since, it is something that Herod who organized the slaughter of the innocents would understand, but not an angel.

I guess, too, that an angel would just naturally back away from the sickening thought that even in communities long exposed to the gospel, people often live on certain streets only if they have the right color. If we had been born of another race, there are dear friends who would at once reject us.

An angel would surely be tempted to back away from the heart that ignores the poverties all around us—and in us—poverties, not only of pocketbook, but of the famished soul.

I righted the louvered wheel, and at once the angels started flying forward again. In this time of the promise, if all of us begin to have in ourselves something of the mind of Christ, it could be that the angels won't think of flying backward again in our generation.

And a Currier-and-Ivesy Christmas to You

The December meeting of the preachers set all the brethren pondering the mysteries of a proper celebration of Christmas. When I expressed a preference for a Christmas all spruce and pine, drifts of snow, nipping cold outside and glowing within, plenty of children on hand, grandfathers and grandmothers in the offing, and the same delight in food that the Bob Cratchits displayed over a goose, there was silence while one of the more learned of the cloth regarded me darkly.

"You," he said in high disdain, "have an entirely Currier-and-Ivesy theology of Christmas."

Come to think of it, that's exactly what it is, I guess, and I would pray the same blessings for you. The reason is that long ago God decided on a Currier-and-Ivesy style of manger with a Child in the midst, and oxen and sheep giving their rapt attention.

Over your head you have "a multitude of the heavenly knighthood," as Wycliffe translates it, for the carols. Suddenly you notice the shepherds finding their way down from the shepherds' field, some wise men climbing down from their camels and bringing gifts. Then notice the warmth somewhere inside you that, as far as I can see from the old masters, is the Child himself.

There are probably people who would settle for an abstract Christmas, just as once there were gnostics who preferred a disembodied Christ. But the Child who lay in Mary's arms was no abstraction. His crying was real. So was his love.

May you have a Currier-and-Ivesy Christmas too.

From an Advent Diary

The December wind is whistling down the chimney and wailing at the parsonage window like all the ghosts who ever sent a shiver up the trembling spine of Scrooge. It is a real Hound-of-the-Baskervilles sort of night that makes you want to pray for all strayed and numbed and snowbound creatures.

I don't know who first introduced the ghosts of Christmas past—probably Dickens—but if your memories are like ours, these are the best ghosts of all. We like to think of Christmas Eves when the four young Webbs were little tads and when their grandfather who always provided the turkey brought a bigger one each year until one Christmas he worked himself up to a thirty-two-pounder. It took a relay of cooks all night to keep the beautiful bird basted with the yummy things that get poured on roasting turkeys.

At the moment the fire is leaping up on the hearth. Two grandchildren are cuddling down for the night.

"Did you have sweet dreams last night?" I ask the next morning, and the four-year-old answers, "Oh, yes!" and tells how she pummeled a boy with the surprising sequel of seeing his big toe turn into an egg. A child Picasso, yet. There are twelve grandchildren now, all very satisfactory. (When you are young you play the dating game. When you are old you play the doting game.)

If you see a plume of smoke blowing over your house, it might well be from our chimney, and it might arrange itself into a scrawl that says, "We love you." That's for Christmas and always.

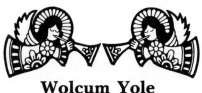

Wolcum Yole

Wolcum be thou hevene king,
Wolcum Yole!

It was an evening late in Advent, and I was trying to sing the medieval carol "Wolcum Yole," but I always look like one of the crooked-mouth people when I pucker up to "wolcum" in the Yuletide. Alice and I were thumbing through an issue of the *New Yorker*. To tell the truth, I was trying to con her into giving me a really spectacular Christmas present.

"See here," I said, "Steuben Glass is offering a handsome crystal paperweight designed to look like the stone from which King Arthur pulled the sword Excalibur. It comes with a sterling silver letter opener that is a broadsword with a gold-bound hilt. Cheap at $585."

"Forget it," Alice said. "You know what happened to Queen Guinevere while Arthur was pulling Excalibur from the stone" (it was easy to see that this Christmas game is one that two can play, and Alice caught on rapidly).

"It would be a lot more sensible," Alice said, "to consider this little number that Cartier has whipped up. It's called Eternal Flame, and it has all the mystery and enchantment of fire captured in this cabochon ruby and diamond necklace and earing ensemble of 18-carat gold. Necklace with flexible pendent, $12,900. Earrings, $3,750."

"Not practical," I demurred. "The cabochon ruby wouldn't go at all with that brown jumper you bought at Sears and Roebuck. But, while we're being practical, I wouldn't mind this rolling clock, an exclusive Gubelin creation. It's for people, it says here, with imagination and a taste for art and beauty. They obviously had me in mind. The clock rolls to a prescribed position daily and gives the date and week. It's the perfect clock to adorn a desk like mine—$1,350, and it's made of zebranowood."

"You know perfectly well," Alice said, "that your desk does not need a zebranowood clock. It's littered so high that men whose wives nag them about their messy dens bring those wives to see your desk, just to take the heat off."

But at this the candles flickered, and we heard the sounds of happy voices at our door. When we flung it wide, fifteen lusty voices broke forth with "O Little Town of Bethlehem" and

"Good Christian Men, Rejoice," carols guaranteed to warm the cockles of your faltering heart forever.

Properly chastened, Alice and I looked at each other, threw the *New Yorker* with Excalibur and the rolling clock into the fire and watched while the flames consumed the lesser gifts.

Olive Oyl and the Christmas Angels

The other evening one of the men in our church learned that his wife had invited her pastor to their home. This left her husband more than a little shaken.

"What," he wanted to know, "can you safely talk to preachers about?"

"Ask him the difference between the cherubim and the seraphim," his wife said helpfully. "They will keep him occupied all evening."

If I consider myself an authority on the distinction between these two orders and have figured out how many angels can safely dance on the head of a pin, it is because I have been entertaining angels *not* unawares at my house, and we are less than a week into Advent.

Alice has long been an admirer of those Christmas angels that our friends assemble out of papier-mâché and paint gold. She spent a morning recently fashioning her first one. When it came hot off the press (or whatever it is you turn angels out on), she looked at the creature ruefully and asked, "What do you think?"

"She's nice," I said, "but she looks like Popeye's girl friend Olive Oyl."

"She *does* look like Olive Oyl," Alice said, "but there is no reason why Olive Oyl can't be an angel too if you want her to be. Maybe she will look better when I get her wings stitched on."

Olive Oyl didn't.

"According to some folks," I said, "angels are always men. Don't you remember the controversy the year the Christmas postage stamp pictured the angel Gabriel in a female form? Lots of people will tell you there aren't any female angels."

"Olive Oyl is," Alice insisted. "You don't have to look like Greta Garbo to be an angel. Besides, you're not one to care what gender angels are."

"She lacks *something*," I protested.

"Pay no attention," Alice said. "Another coat of paint will do wonders for her."

"Where will you hang her?"

"Top of the Christmas tree, of course."

So Christmas is coming, Christmas art is blooming at our house, and Olive Oyl is on the shelf drying, proud to think she is going to be our Christmas angel. Olive Oyl cannot tell the difference between the cherubim and the seraphim—I guess she is merely a common or garden variety of angel—but that is all it takes to have a proper kind of Christmas.

The Madonna of the Salt Water Taffy

"Go hence and cool thyself an hour!" I declaimed, doing a roaring performance of Matthew Arnold's ballad "Saint Brandan."

"Did I miss something?" Alice asked.

It was Christmas Eve and colder than the statue of the iced-up nobleman in *Don Giovanni*.

"It appears," I said, "that Saint Brandan was scouring around in the frigid north in search of an earthly paradise one Christmas Eve, when he overtook Judas Iscariot floating on an iceberg. Judas Iscariot was cooling off from his previous year in the hot dominions of Satan. Seems that he once tossed his cloak to a beggar, and as a reward the Lord allows him to cool off every Christmas Eve."

"It *is* a cold Christmas Eve," Alice admitted.

The thought struck us simultaneously: a block down the street loomed the orange roofs of a Howard Johnson restaurant. We flung on our coats and stepped forth for a cup of coffee.

As we entered the restaurant a strange, rotating eye-grabber got our attention. It was a pyramid of boxes of salt water taffy, topped by a dismal little crèche with the Holy Family and several oxen and sheep that had had a hard time of it in Christmas past. The Virgin Mary, in cheap plaster with the colors of her blue robe flaking off, dominated this giddy heap of goodies.

Never one to boggle at the merest hints divinity displays, I watched the Virgin Mary as she spun dizzily around. One could only ponder the innocent motive that had installed her there. Could this have been the very crèche that Howard Johnson had under his Christmas tree as a little boy? Any restaurateur who could project hundreds of orange roofs to gladden the traveler's eye in the dark mid-winter would surely have had the imagination in his boyhood to be turned on by a plaster Joseph and Mary and Christ Child.

But only a restaurant manager whose business it is to catch the eye of the public would have thought of placing the crèche on top of a pyramid of salt water taffy and setting the whole business spinning. Still, maybe this is exactly where a crèche belongs, for Christmas has a way of adopting all fugitive and elfin things—stockings hung by the chimney with care, the Nutcracker Suite, medieval carols that evoke the time of wonder, whole armies of gingerbread men baking in fragrant ovens—and of course the salt water taffy.

I cast another glance at the Holy Family whirling incessantly around, and I could only decide that this is just as it should be, for they were looking out in every direction from their little Bethlehem on top of the salt water taffy.

Already they were conjuring miracles. Black December nights were alight with trees shouting glory. Faces in the restaurant were growing gentler as "Silent Night" floated down on us from the ceiling. In the candlelight there was something tender in the eyes of young lovers as they reached out and touched each other's hands.

An incredible miracle was spinning there before me. I drank my hot chocolate in the presence of the Holy Family, and, although usually a Scrooge to the very core, surprised myself by giving the waitress an incredible tip. When the Holy Family has its eyes on you, you have to be at your best.

Er—That Name Again?

It is approaching that special time of year when the holly and the ivy are vying for a place in the sun. There is only one drawback—those Christmas greetings that omit the surname of the sender. For years at our house we have been receiving a Christmas greeting from Rexford and Molly.

"Who," I ponder, "are Rexford and Molly?"

A puzzled look spreads over Alice's face.

"You used to know the dean of a cathedral named Rexford," she hazards.

"That Rexford," I answer scornfully, "was too stingy to send his own grandmother a Christmas greeting."

We stare at each other helplessly as we have done for several Christmases past. Rexford and Molly? At what crossroads did we first encounter this loving pair whose surname escapes us? Is it a game of one-upsmanship they are playing in order to make us feel remiss in not sending *them* a card?

Then, too, there are those dear friends you made thirty years ago whom you haven't seen since. You are bound to run into them at Christmas concerts. They bear down on you like a windjammer, smile at you with beamish joy, lay hold of your lapel, and taunt, "You *don't* remember us, do you?"

No, you don't. But they are so eager to be remembered that it would be a crime to admit the truth.

"Ah!" you say, making a stab at a plausible guess, "You are the ones who had the beautiful grandchild." At this they curl their lips and reply, *"We* are the ones who had the *seven* beautiful grandchildren!" No help there.

On one occasion a woman hailed me from her bed as I passed her room in the hospital. "I'll bet you don't remember my name," she gloated. "You called on someone who was in the same ward with me every day for two weeks, and still you don't remember my name."

A rare inspiration struck me. "I'll bet you don't remember my name either," I hazarded. A puzzled look overspread her face. "Why!" she said, "You're—you're—?"

"It's nice seeing you again," I said and vanished out of the room.

It seems likely that John the Elder, who wrote the book of Revelation, had a poor memory for names. He makes a number of allusions to people whose names appear on their foreheads where they can be plainly seen.

What a good place to have your name! People who mourn their lack of total recall would brighten up at once when they met you. When you go to heaven, heaven would be a more comfortable place because you would know everybody at once.

Even the angel Gabriel would not have to identify himself to you. The cherubim and seraphim would cease to be merely anonymous inhabitants of the thronged air. Maybe they would have names like Jane or Nellie or Joe or Pete, and you could call them by their names and feel at home with them at once.

No doubt Rexford and Molly will be there too with their names shining brightly in their foreheads, and you will not mind moseying up to them and passing the time of day. This will be one of the greatest things about the kingdom of heaven: you will know everyone's name.

But there will be one you will know even though his name may not be written on his forehead. You will recognize him because you have known him all along. Those who looked forward to his first appearance called him by many names— Wonderful Counselor, the Mighty God, Everlasting Father, the Prince of Peace. And those who looked back at his coming also knew him by many names—Master and Emmanuel, Savior and Lord.

Unstatistical Methods

It was the afternoon of the university's great Christmas concert. Massed choirs were squaring off to sing the "Hallelujah Chorus." At this point a belated student sauntered in with a treatise on statistical methods under her arm. Final examinations were in the offing, and this earnest seeker of the world's knowledge was not about to waste any time while Handel was bringing all heaven down.

I could see the student bracing herself against the glory as the treaty on statistics began to occupy her mind. But, of course, this is why the wise men saw the star and Herod did not. A census was in progress, and he was so busy counting heads he missed the important event, which was the fact that heaven was touching earth into a new brightness.

Suppose the Virgin Mary had been occupied with statistics when she received the great announcement. "Oh, no!" Mary would have protested to the angel Gabriel. "Statistics are all against anything like this happening. The probability of God's making a simple maid like me an instrument of his peace is a zillion to one."

Or suppose that wonderful old party Simeon, who had been haunting the temple for many years hoping to catch a glimpse of the promised Messiah before his eyes failed, had consulted a text on statistical methods. "The chances of my being around for such an event is .0000099," Simeon would have said. "I won't bother to visit the temple today." Because of his obsession with improbability, he would have missed seeing the face of the Child. He could never have said, "Mine eyes have seen thy salvation."

And we? With our computers and our pocket calculators, we are able to launch men to the moon, but all these instruments put together fail to inform us of the one Star that is the light of all our seeing.

The fiddles are tuning up for the *Messiah,* and the face of Handel rises before me. He is blowing on his hands in the cold room in London where he is composing this music that will never let the heart alone. He raises his head to peer through the darkness and to say, as he did when the inspiration seized him, "I thought I did see all heaven open and the great God before me." Ever since then the "Hallelujah Chorus" has blown the mind—and you cannot get any of it into the statistics.

Christmas Letters
from Your Grandchildren

Some of the nicest Christmas presents are the letters you receive from your grandchildren. The thought of Christmas turns any child's thoughts toward the *real meaning* of Christmas, which is not just an airy sentiment, but something you can unwrap.

Spelling never seems to get in the way of the bursts of affection these letters express, as in this from one of mine.

> I hop you are felling well.
> I hop you like my lettler.

You learn to write like this if you learned to read from Dick and Jane ("Jane, see the cat." "Dick, see Jane see the cat"). The letter continues:

> I hop you had a nice Thanksgiving.
> Have you been going to church I have.
> My mother bought the Christmas prents
> for everybuddy we no.
> P.S. Wirte back please.
>> Love,
>>> Jennifer

A letter like this can warm your heart for a month of Sundays. It can immunize you against grinches that steal Christmas, because the whole gospel is in a letter like Jennifer's. It is God becoming real in gifts that grab the heart with their mystery from Bethlehems whose sages show up with absurd offerings like frankincense and myrrh. So I am going to "wirte" to Jennifer and pray that "everybuddy we no" gets lots of Christmas "prents."

The Cardinal and the Wren

A little gift shop called the Apple Tree has recently opened in our town. Enter its friendly door, and you think you are in Bethlehem sniffing the frankincense and myrrh the magi brought to the manger. Alice and I are sauntering into the shop at the same moment, but we did not plan it that way. Since Christmas is drawing near, it is not hard to guess why we have come, but, of course, we are both pretending just to be casually looking in.

Oddly, we are both attracted to the table where there is an assortment of birds carved in walnut by an old woodcarver down in the Appalachians. We each keep turning away from the table as if we have something else in mind, but Alice knows that as soon as her back is turned I will lay aside for her the little wren with its head cocked as if it knew from the first it was destined for her Christmas stocking. And when I look again the handsome cardinal has disappeared, and I know she has had a clerk confiscate it for me.

We do our best to make a secret of our small purchases, but suspicion runs high, and there is little doubt what we are going to give each other. Come Christmas morning, we shall be pretending that we are completely surprised by our walnut birds.

After all, Christmas means taking the one you love by surprise, and this is what God did to us all at Bethlehem. This must be the reason why Alice and I, each by a different route, happened in at the Apple Tree at the same moment and found the wren and the cardinal. When December snows lie deep, our walnut birds will be a promise that spring is coming, and with it a return of all the wrens and cardinals to Brookview Court.

On Not Finding a Baby on Your Doorstep

The sun had barely risen when Alice peeked out of the window.

"Remarkable!" she said. "Someone has left a baby carriage on our walk."

"Did anyone leave a baby on our doorstep?" I asked apprehensively.

"I don't see one," Alice said. "But there is no doubt about it, there is an empty baby carriage headed toward our door. Maybe somebody is trying to tell us something."

"Maybe it's an *invisible* baby on our doorstep," I countered.

"You can't do very much with an invisible baby," Alice said. "None of *our* children was ever invisible. When they were little they usually became visible at dawn and stayed visible all day."

"I wonder what would happen if there *were* an invisible baby on our doorstep," I said.

"You're always quoting something about God's leaving a Baby on the doorstep of the world," Alice said.

"If we had eyes to see it," I said, "maybe that is what God is doing all the time—leaving invisible babies on doorsteps and hoping the goodman of the house and his goodwife will take them in."

"Such as—?" Alice lifted a wary eyebrow at my speculation.

"Well, the hungry of the world," I said, "because there are millions of hungry children. You can't see their faces for the numbers, so they're invisible to you. But if you will take the time to imagine one fair Child in swaddling clothes on your doorstep, it won't be long before your eyes are opened to see another and another, till you know that the earth is God's footstool, and you have to do something for the hungry ones your generosities can reach.

"Or you think of the hospitals and homes our church has helped to support in other lands. You can't see the faces of the multitudes for whom Christ cares. But if you had an invisible Baby on your doorstep, you would be able to imagine at least *one* face or hear *one* famished cry or see at least *one* hand stretched toward you in a silent appeal for your love. Before you knew it you would squelch the Scrooge within you and join with your friends to make His healing presence real.

"Or . . ." But at this, someone came to claim the mysterious baby carriage and made off with it.

That is how Alice and I put the invisible Child in the baby carriage and sent him on his way to be left at another doorstep—and another and another—until all the world is blessed by a knowledge of him who is remembered best for having taken little children in his arms.

On Not Exchanging Christmas Presents

It was the day after Christmas. Everyone was out exchanging gifts because Christmas always triggers you to give your true-love-true some handsome article of clothing—always in the wrong size. Nothing makes a man more human. It convinces women of the helplessness of men and makes them want to mother the poor chaps.

In my own case, I have worked out a system so that I don't have to exchange anything after Christmas. I get my family to give me the books I had coveted all along, so while the rest of the world is plowing through the snow to the department store, I am seated by the fire getting deeper and deeper into some great reading.

Thinking how much of my wealth is in something that does not need exchanging, it occurred to me that most of us are continually being given something so much to our liking that we would not exchange it for the world—love. However it comes to you, love from someone you care for deeply is something you do not have to take back the day after. It grows and grows until your heart is fair to bursting. It takes only one person to love you to make you feel like that.

Or, count on your fingers the ten friends dearest to you, who have stood by you through thick and thin—you would not exchange them for a bushel of gold and frankincense and myrrh.

Or, take the faith you began to breathe, perhaps with the warmth of your father's house as a child, or that came to you afterward because God has his hand upon you—nobody is going to persuade you to exchange this the day after Christmas.

The day after Christmas the young lady who was given the ten lords a-leaping found they were now ten lords a-limping and sent them packing to the store where you buy leaping lords. But the love that prompted such an imaginative gift she surely kept forever.

Needed: An *Un*decorating Committee

Advent is a pleasant anticipation for most of us, with Christmas trees springing up everywhere and a glow in the heart celebrating the amazing ways in which God is always taking us by surprise. It is a shining you see in the eyes of youth as they hang the greens.

But one ghost of Christmas past is another matter. While it is exciting to put up the decorations for the great celebration, it is sadder than the eyes of Einstein to take them down afterward. The hardest thing to find in a church is an *un*decorating committee to put out the candles, stow the mistletoe, and dismantle the splendors for another season.

Still, when you come to think of it, the *un*decorating committee is just as important as anyone else. You cannot go caroling or give presents forever, for there is

> a time to seek, and a time to lose;
> a time to keep, and a time to cast away. (Ecclesiastes 3:6)

Life is not all ecstasy, lest at last even ecstasy become tame. Those elations we feel at the supreme moments of our life yield at last to a more sober order, and for our good. The Spirit of him who is our Lord enters into us and seeks the deeper levels of the soul, residing there as an ineffable presence and a final hope, yet seldom calling attention to himself.

After Christmas is over and the lights go out, you may feel glum at first, but then you remember it doesn't take much of anything to have what Christmas is (although a pair of new skates helps in cold climates). All it really takes is the faith that beyond all the hurtful things is a Love so great it always writes the final word.

If you are beginning to feel dispirited as you dismantle your Christmas tree and put away the angel, be of good cheer. The Christ you have celebrated will be in your midst all your days in the toils and temptations and in the unheralded strengths you will know in each day's most pressing need.

The Tower of Babble

If I am already shuddering a little at the return of Advent, it is not because of the hanging of the greens, the decoration of Christmas trees, or that sparkling air of goodwill that pervades the heart, turns Main Street into fairyland, and adds a new piquancy to the greetings of old friends. All this I love.

The lurking suspicion that not all is well has to do with "It Came Upon the Midnight Clear," which we shall all be singing soon. A glorious hymn, that one, but with one word that trips us all before we know it—the word "Babel" with a long *a*.

And ever o'er its Bābel sounds
The blessed angels sing.

It is at this point that the unwitting in the United Kingdoms sing "babble" instead of "Babel." As I see it, this is the only drawback to Advent—the incessant babble. One is sometimes be-Jingle-Belled and be-Scrooged and be-eggnogged one time too many. There must be something one can do to make a place of stillness immune to babble during Advent.

For example, turn to the lovely old Scriptures in St. Matthew and St. Luke that tell of the Child who was born to save his people from their sins. Or add to your library of Christmas books a minor classic that was meant for reading by the fire some evening when the scene outside your window is a reproduction of your favorite Christmas card. Or listen to an ancient yuletide carol. Or think for a little time about your church and how across the years, without any pressure except the love of God it has drawn to itself a communion of kindred spirits to abide in Christ.

There are ways and ways and a Way through all the "babble sounds" to find your way to Christmas—and on to the heart of the Most High.

The Children Were Hung by the Chimney with Care

Christmas in the United States has become a breeder of mental depression and infantile behavior and a reminder of an unhappy past for some people, says a psychiatric research team. . . . It can be a headache for people who don't want to play the holiday game as it has developed in American culture, the researchers added.

O Tannenbaum! O Tannenbaum!
I feel an apprehensive qualm.
As Christmas morning zeros in
I loathe my kith, detest my kin.
Beshrew the ivy and the holly—
They leave me quite unnerved, by golly,
And Santa with his antlered eight
I'd willingly exterminate.
My yuletide mood is deeply Stygian
And sours my hard-acquired religion.
Allergic to the mistletoe,
I find I also can forgo
The lilting, ancient Yuletide carol
And Christmas throngs in gay apparel.
Evoke not for the likes of me
A partridge in an old pear tree.
Amahl and his night visitors
I'd consign to the inquisitors,
And inconsiderately I'd toss
Out your old friend King Wenceslaus.
Let ribbon candy go unsung,
It cloys upon the coated tongue.
Bah, humbug to whoever would
See all his family ties renewed.

My scorn of Christmas joys is huge.
So ends this lamentation—
                                    Scrooge.

But soft! A mood a shade less gruesome
Reanimates this churlish bosom;
For now a kindly folk appear
Who sing the sagging heart good cheer
With frosty breath, and what is more,
Come trooping gladly to your door.
They make the starry welkin ring
With "Hark! The Herald Angels Sing."
"It Came Upon the Midnight Clear"
Shatters our crystal chandelier.
They'd like to see a flowing bowl
But settle for "The First Noel."
They've come to set the old world right,
And it's no longer silent night.

So, welcome friends who loudly sing
The Child who is our Christmas king;
And welcome all whose merry din
Has helped to usher Christmas in.

The Rembrandt Effect

It would not be Christmas in our village church if Miss O'Shaughnessy did not bring all Bethlehem down the aisle on Christmas Eve. Tabards are always back in style for occasions like this. Rakish crowns cut from cardboard and finished off with gold paper adorn the wise men she recruits from the small fry who are helpless in her firm command of the Christmas dramas.

The wise men in their bathrobes are always a cut above our shepherds, who have to content themselves with costumes fashioned from burlap bags. As the shepherds oar themselves down the aisle on their shepherds' crooks there is a faint odor of grists from our local feed mill, so that we have an authentic sense of earthy things about us, and this is all to the good.

Joseph, usually an awkward lanky lad, always looks a little shifty-eyed as if he were planning an escape. He stands self-consciously behind the Virgin Mary. She is bound to upstage him from the start, but the poor fellow expects this and shortly becomes resigned to his fate.

It is the Virgin Mary with whom Miss O'Shaughnessy takes the most pains. Mary is a girl with innocence written over her face as she sits gazing a little blankly into hay in the manger.

"Be sure," Miss O'Shaughnessy always instructs the cast, "that there is a light bulb burning in the manger before anyone arrives for the pageant, so that when the Virgin Mary gazes down into the hay the light will flood up into her face as it does in the old masters. What we are after is the Rembrandt effect."

But, of course, there are Christmas Eves when little things like this slip your mind. One year the Virgin Mary arrived in the chancel, settled herself to gaze down into the manger, and found that no one had turned on the light. Anxious for the Rembrandt effect, she reached into the manger and threw the switch on the decrepit light socket hidden there. Click! You could hear the sound of it to the back pew, but no light came on. Someone had forgotten to plug it in.

At this moment a woman in the congregation has an idea. She had come across muddy fields, lighted on her way by a flashlight, one of those silvered affairs as long as your arm. She resolutely marched up to the chancel and laid her flashlight in the manger. The Virgin Mary took the hint, reached into the manger to turn it on—*only it didn't turn on either.* Poor Mary had to play the scene in the gloom the way the original Virgin Mary did in the cold of that manger without any illumination except, of course, from that remarkable star that was shining down through a hole in the roof over the place where the young Child lay.

I guess that you cannot always depend on the Rembrandt effect when Christmas comes. There will be years when Christmas comes with all the lights blazing, but it will also come to shadowed thresholds dark with fears. It weaves its lovely spell, not only when your children are young and all your dearest gather about you, but also when you have grown old and sup alone, remembering how much you have lost with the lost years, and like Cleopas and his companion in the dusk at Emmaus, you find an unseen guest is breaking bread at your lonely table.

Sing, Hosts of Heaven

Sing, hosts of heaven and children all,
The Holy Child we sing—
Behold the lowly cattle stall
That cradles Christ your King.

From frosty byre and upland wild
Come, shepherds, find the way
That leads to Bethlehem and the Child
Asleep upon the hay.

Remote as in a dream we see
Beneath the starlight's glow
The shadows of the star-mazed three
Who follow through the snow.

For you who walk a frozen earth
This then shall be the sign:
The swaddled Christ Child at his birth
With oxen and with kine.

Sing, sons of men and hosts on high,
Lift every voice and sing—
God's love pours through the cloven sky,
The Christ of God is King.

And sing, ye children, sing with power,
Your little Lord is born:
For you shall blossom as your dower
The white and flowering thorn.

Sing, Host of Heaven

Wheaton P. Webb

Carl L. Snyder

1. Sing, hosts of heav-en and chil - dren all, The ho - ly child we sing.

Be - hold the low - ly cat - tle stall That cra - dles Christ your King.

2. From frost - y byre and up - land wild, Come,
3. Re - mote as in a dream we see Be -

shep - herds, find the way That leads to Beth - le - hem
neath the star - light's glow The shad - ows of the

and the child A - sleep up - on the hay.
star - mazed three Who fol - low through the snow.

We Interrupt This Program . . .

It has happened times without number: you push back the cares of the world and are settling down to watch your favorite program on television. The program is working itself up to a climax and has all your attention when the screen blacks out and a voice fraught with ominous overtones announces, "We interrupt this program . . ."

The announcement is always of disaster. Some slaughter of the innocents has occurred: a bridge has collapsed, war has leaped across another border. Whatever the calamity, it chills you to the bone to realize that the security into which you had been lulled by the program is a fantasy, and you are back where you started, facing all that can go wrong in the heart.

Nevertheless, this is not the only kind of interruption we have known. Sometimes a stillness has fallen on us, and we have heard the God of all our high believing say, "We interrupt this program . . ." We were perhaps the last to expect that it could happen to the likes of us, immersed as we were in the settled years when everything was going to be as it had ever been. Yet it happened.

This is at the heart of all we mean by Christmas. The great and loving God of our fathers has interrupted the program. Just when we are lowest there is "a sunset touch." All heaven breaks through with the promise, "Behold, a virgin shall conceive and bear a son, and his name shall be called God-with-us."

Hope springs anew, not the flawed optimism so easily undone by the accidents of time, but confidence born of a faith that reposes its trust in the God who is the Father of our Lord Jesus Christ.

A man who tunes some of the great church organs of this country told me that he once found a message which an organist had left for him, "I've done all I can with this instrument." When we examine ourselves we are often tempted to pin up a similar sign. But God is not through with us yet. If we allow the Master's hand to touch us, his love will put us back in tune.

Sometimes he does this when we pray. Sometimes he does it when we live for him with undeviating purpose. Sometimes he comes, all the doors being shut, and breathes his "Peace, be still" over the muted reeds of our numbed experience, and in his hands the instrument begins to play its part in the prelude to a new greatness. Just when we were ready to conclude that our famished being would never again give voice to the deep diapasons of the soul's exultant music, our Lord comes and touches the failed stops with his healing presence, and we awaken to all that the ancient proclamation can intend. "Behold, a virgin shall conceive and bear a son, and his name shall be called God-with-us."

Something unanticipated has visited us, and we interrupt this program to make room in our hearts to receive him.

And yet—it shakes the heart to ponder what would have become of us if God had not interrupted the program of the hopeless years, if the first Christmas had never dawned, and if we had had to live in a world to which Christ had not come.

It is not difficult to imagine what a world without Christ's presence would have been, for we have seen that world in all its brutality. In the days of the Second World War just a week before Christmas 1942, Joseph Goebbels, Hitler's propaganda minister, made this entry in his diary:

The Christmas program for radio and the press has been submitted for my okay. We are limiting ourselves to only a few broadcasts and editorials dealing exclusively with Christmas. It won't do for the people in these difficult times to fall too much for the sentimental magic of these festival days.

There *is* sentiment, honest as the heart, that prompts "these festival days" when Christmas comes. It is a sentiment compounded of love put into a story that can be told only the way the Gospels tell it. Every year when Christmas dawns in all the homes that honor Christ, there is renewed a Christian mystery that no propaganda minister can control.

God interrupted the program of King Herod and his slaughter of the innocents. He interrupted the thousand year *reich* that was eclipsing all that was compassionate and gentle and human. His spirit interrupts "the dark inheritance of hate" that has held so much of the earth in thrall. When God interrupts the program, his interruption takes over the program, and Christmas becomes more than a lyric interlude in the bleak midwinter of our years.

Instant Christmas

"Maybe Christmas," he thought, *"doesn't* come from a store."
"Maybe Christmas . . . perhaps . . . means a little bit more!"
—Dr. Seuss: *How the Grinch Stole Christmas*

It was a Monday morning in December when I headed for a shopping mall. At precisely one minute before ten o'clock I arrived at the doors of a great complex of stores that constituted a city in itself. The doors were locked. Presently a clock struck the hour. As I stared the metal gates that guarded the entrance to a department store went clanging up and a loud-speaker began to boom out "The Twelve Days of Christmas."

From nowhere clerks began to appear and a happy bustle of

shoppers poured through the doors. Like a flash, the store had turned on instant Christmas. A spirit of goodwill began to reign—the kind that reigns when you have money jingling in your pocket.

And then the thought: in three weeks the shelves of the stores will be emptied. Exhausted clerks will trudge home for Christmas Eve glassy-eyed with weariness. Someone will push a switch, turn off "The Twelve Days of Christmas," and the season will be instantly over.

Of course it will be over if it is a season that can be turned on and off like a tap. It will be over if it cannot carry on after the shelves are empty, all the presents bought, and all the money spent. It will be over if you expect the eggnog to hold out forever.

Fortunately there are those who all along have been in on the secret: You cannot turn Christmas on or off by throwing a switch. This is because love is a bottomless pocket in the robes of the Most High.

The Short Christmas Dinner

Again the year was coming full circle. The wind was whistling around the gables of the parsonage, but the fire on the hearth was making Christmas Eve cosy. Soon the gray possession of sleep would be overtaking the house, and the children be nestled all snug in their beds.

Alice was knitting the final mitten of the season, while I drowsed over a volume so ancient that the leather binding, smelling of long attention from mice in musty cupboards, was covering my hands with a brown powder.

It was the autobiography of James Lackington, the eighteenth-century London bookseller who through one of John Wesley's people had got in touch with a promising situation in Featherstone Street.

"Look here!" I said, coming to life, "James Lackington must have been a spiritual ancestor of mine; he could never resist a bargain in old books."

"Don't tell *me!*" Alice said, looking up at the piles of books spilling from every table in the room.

"A man after my own heart," I insisted. "Let me read you what happened to him on a Christmas Eve at the time the American Revolution was warming up—"

"He was off mousing around in bookshops?" Alice guessed.

"Exactly," I said. "Hear him now:"

Nor did I forget the old book-shops: but frequently added an old book to my small collection: and I really have often purchased books with the money that should have been expended in purchasing something to eat; a striking instance of which follows:

At the time we were purchasing household goods, we kept ourselves very short of money, and on Christmas-eve we had but half-a-crown left to buy a Christmas dinner. My wife desired that I would go to market, and purchase this festival dinner, and off I set for that purpose; but in the way I saw an old book-shop, and I could not resist the temptation of going in.

"I shudder to anticipate," Alice interjected.

"I fear you are getting warm." I said, "But to continue:"

—intending only to expend sixpence or ninepence out of my half-crown. But I stumbled upon Young's *Night Thoughts*—forgot my dinner—down went the half-crown—and I hastened home, vastly delighted with the acquisition. When my wife asked me where was our Christmas dinner? I told her it was in my pocket.—"In your pocket," said she, "that is a strange place.

How could you think of stuffing a joint of meat into your pocket?" I assured her that it would take no harm. But as I was in no haste to take it out, she began to be more particular, and inquired what I had got, &c. On which I began to harangue on the superiority of intellectual pleasures over sensual gratifications, and observed that the brute creation enjoyed the latter in a much higher degree than man. And that a man, that was not possessed of intellectual enjoyments, was but a two-legged brute.

"The cad!" Alice exclaimed, dropping a stitch.

I was proceeding in this strain: "And so," said she, "instead of buying a dinner, I suppose you have, as you have done before, been buying books with the money?" I confessed I had bought Young's *Night Thoughts:* "And I think," said I, "that I have acted wisely, for had I bought a dinner, we should have eaten it to-morrow, and the pleasure would have been soon over:
  'But in the volumes of the mighty dead,
    We feast on joys to vulgar minds unknown.'
Should we live fifty years longer, we shall have the *Night Thoughts* to feast upon." This was too powerful an argument to admit of any further debate; in short, my wife was convinced. Down I sat, and began to read with as much enthusiasm as the good doctor possessed when he wrote it; and so much did it excite my attention as well as my approbation, that I retained the greater part of it in my memory.

"A likely story!" Alice sniffed. "And what an imposter he was to argue 'the superiority of intellectual pleasure over sensual gratifications' when the alternative was an empty stomach on Christmas Day. There are times when there is no substitute for a goose."
"When?"
"When the Bob Cratchits are about to sit down to their Christmas feast, and Scrooge's stony heart has melted, and Tiny Tim is piping, 'God bless us, every one!'"

"Still," I argued, unwilling to leave well enough alone, "think of the consolation our bookseller took from his *Night Thoughts.*

"Fiddlesticks!" Alice said. "There are moments in life you have to seize on the wing, and Christmas is one of them—like the manna in the wilderness that was good only if you gathered it while it was fresh. That James Lackington! If he had lived in the wilderness with the Hebrew people, he would have spent forty years *reading* about the manna instead of rushing out in a fine careless rapture and gathering some for his Christmas feast, and so would have put the miracle the Lord offered him at one remove.

"Because this is what Christmas really is: it's letting yourself go in an unpremeditated fling that lets all your taste buds come out swinging at the thought of a roast goose. So, if you have any plans for investing in *Night Thoughts* instead of in a very respectable goose that will simmer in my Christmas oven and float heavenly odors up from the parsonage kitchen; if—"

But at this the log on the fire settled more comfortably into the grate as if an argument had been won—and with the promise that Christmas would be rich in fragrances beyond the power of old leatherbound books to match.

On Recovering from the Dramas of Christmas

You do not have to be told what your friends have in mind when they write in their Christmas letter: "All six of us are recovering from the presentation of *The Little Angel*." It is no doubt true that directors of nativity tableaus are an endangered species.

My mind goes back to the dress rehearsal of a Christmas pageant presented in the auditorium of our village school. The curtains opened on a small Bethlehem straight out of a Renaissance painting. Mary gazed fondly at the Child in the manger. Joseph, older than time in his beard, stood protectingly over her. A hearty ringing of camel bells introduced three wise men as resplendent as sultans. If the director of this small drama had known, he would have stopped it while he was ahead.

Enter, four small boys in their coats of many colors, arriving breathlessly from the shepherds' field in order to frame the Holy Family.

The difficulty was that the shepherds were wearing their costumes over their ordinary clothing, and under the lights the heat was overpowering. Suddenly the first of the four shepherds fell over in a dead faint at the feet of the Virgin Mary. There was nothing for it but to ring down the curtain, apply the spirits of ammonia, fan the shepherd back to consciousness, and drag him off the stage.

The curtain went up with only three shepherds left to do the honors, but at this juncture a second shepherd succumbed to the heat and promptly fainted. Again the curtain fell, the spirits of ammonia were produced, the swooning shepherd opened his fluttering lids, and was dragged off before the curtain went up again.

It was not a day for shepherds. There were only two left, and their faces were gray with apprehension. Clunk! The third shepherd collapsed, and a rapid curtain caught the stage manager rushing back on stage with his faithful bottle of spirits of ammonia.

Doggedly the tableau continued. For a final time the curtain rose, and there, where someone had forgotten to remove it was—the spirits of ammonia beside the frankincense and myrrh the wise men had left.

There will always be those who argue that spirits of ammonia are out of place in the company of the gifts of the magi. But put me down as one who honors the way the bottle of spirits of ammonia made its way to the Holy Nativity. What frankincense and myrrh are incapable of doing, the spirits of ammonia did: it brought the breathless shepherds back to consciousness and sent them on their way rejoicing back to whatever needed their attention. It too was a Christmas gift, prosaic surely, and not likely to make its way into the canon of your better Christmas stories, but doing its best in a quiet way to serve—and the Virgin Mary would be the first to approve of that.

The Christmas Serpent

"Won't you," the personnel director of the hospital asked, "come over and tell a Christmas story to the children's ward?"

Never one to refuse to spin a story to children, I chose that old favorite "The Third Lamb" and set off. The story is as tender as they come—poor children in a Tyrolean village, a perfectly splendid old wood-carver who knows the way to a child's heart through his knack for carving children's toys, and, best of all, a vision of "the Fair Boy," the Christ Child whom he meets in the mountains. Who could fail with a story as good as this? It needs only a stillness of the heart for it all to become very real.

When I arrived in the corridor outside the children's ward, pandemonium was in progress. A magician had the children screaming with delight. His routine ended with palming off the ace of spades on a small boy. The boy looked at the card and returned it to the magician, who tossed the whole deck into a wicker basket. All eyes were concentrated on the basket.

Slowly the lid began to move and a fiendishly repelling cobra raised its head higher and higher out of the basket. In the mouth of the serpent was—*the ace of spades!*

Thunderous and continuous applause.

"Mr. Webb will now tell the Christmas story."

Alas, who can compete with a serpent as wily as the one the magician deployed? I looked darkly at the man, who normally was only an innocent director of a church choir, and floundered into my story that had never failed me before. It failed me now. The serpent had outwitted me completely, captivated my audience, and left me breathing hard. The tender mysticism of "The Third Lamb" was shattered beyond repair. There was no retrieving such a sacred moment as I had felt once before when telling the story to some lonely orphans seated around a Christmas tree. The atmosphere for "The Third Lamb" had vanished.

But, of course, Christmas isn't one to wait for proper atmospheres, or it never would have dawned in the first place. The serpent was there—had always been there, right from the beginning, had organized Herod—Old King Horrid, my kids used to call him—for the slaughter of the innocents.

But Christmas kept coming. It kept coming across the years, sometimes to Christians hiding in the catacombs, or to prisoners like Hans Lilje during the Hitler years. Always and always, someone has been willing to do the will of the serpent, to invent a new poison gas or conceive a weapon so terrible that "the black spool of war" begins unwinding again.

You would like to isolate Christmas from all the realities that numb the heart, but it refuses to let itself be dissipated into easy sentiments. The heavenly host that hovered over Bethlehem on the night of the star refused to play the role of "beautiful but ineffectual angels beating through the luminous void their wings in vain," because they were bound for a rough field where certain poor shepherds watched their flocks by night.

It has always been like this, Christmas has. I was once present at a madrigal concert of the Renaissance Singers of Bowling Green State University. The concert was held in the great gallery of the Toledo Art Museum. The walls of the room were hung with magnificent Nativities by Rubens and other old masters.

The rapturous young voices of students in Renaissance dress, accompanied by ancient lutes added a great Christmas glory to the already stunning splendors of the gallery. And then the serpent—I had been blinded to his presence at first—but slowly my eyes focused on the large painting behind the singers. Salome has brought in the head of John the Baptist, and from a table the grisly face, its eyes wild, held your rapt attention while you became momentarily blind to the Rubens nativity shining from another wall, forgot the Renaissance Singers and the occasion of their concert. "It is a bad world . . ." Cyprian wrote in his "Epistle to Donatus."

True enough, and the serpent has had his way with us long enough. With an effort I began to listen to the music. The lyricism of the madrigals laid hold like a seizure of eagles. No, you could not depend on Christmas to wait till earth was no longer hard as iron or till the serpent was no more. Christmas was bound to come, not least to lonely souls who were in possession of no gifts but the Spirit's ancient power.

I thought of something that that good Concord worthy, Bronson Alcott had entered in his journal on Christmas Eve 1875. Discouragements had often marshalled their battalions at his door. He had had to close his Boston school when he refused to exclude a black student and white parents had withdrawn their children in protest. All his life he had known little but poverty. But it is Christmas Eve and a kindly hand is rapping at his door: "Emerson calls and spends an hour in my study. When friends are few and Christmas gifts are rare, I may count this visit as a Christmas Eve gift, and take pleasure as well as pride in the friendship."

"Emerson calls—" And with the fidelities of such a friend on

Christmas Eve, the serpent is no longer in possession of the ace of spades. Yes, and suddenly it is a good world, Donatus!

The Star That Stops for a Child

It is late on a frosty night in December, and Alice and I are looking up at something. On the roof of the hospital a beautiful star is shining the way a star ought to when it comes to rest over the place where a young child lies. Follow the rays of the star down the roof, remembering a stable, and you are in the maternity ward where another young mother has given birth to a beautiful child.

Beneath the star there are birth pangs tonight, but something greater than the pain is up there on the roof shedding its beams abroad. Now you are remembering that other star that stopped for a Child. "It came to rest over the place where the young child was" (Matthew 2:9).

I have no doubt that a star like the one that paused over Bethlehem, or the one beaming its rays down from the roof of our hospital, shines with a special brilliance for young people like Anne and William whose first child was born this Christmas Eve. William has been present to hold her hand during her labor and to murmur, "There! There!" with all the helplessness of a man who suspects he is really in the way.

"William is such a dear," Anne tells us. "He suffered sympathetic labor pains."

"What did the doctor do for William?" I ask her.

"Oh! He didn't do anything for William. The doctor gave me sedation—and William went to sleep!"

Even a star on the hospital roof is bound to shine a little more proudly for the Annes and Williams of this odd old world. If a star could purse its lips and make droll remarks, it would surely do this when it sees someone like William, all solicitation, dozing off. William will wake at last to a baby's low cry, and the miracle of birth we honor at Bethlehem will renew itself in homes where young parents are painting a nursery pink or blue and preparing to welcome's God's great gift.

Christmas for a Medieval Lady

I do not know how it occurred to me—perhaps it was dressing up for the Boar's Head Madrigal Costume Dinner a week before Christmas. For the occasion Alice had attired herself in a smashing green dress with slit sleeves that would have made Queen Elizabeth I and her court envious. This was topped off with a steeple hat two feet tall made of matching material with a trailing veil. Bewitching was the only word for it, though it *did* tend to remind one of a dunce cap. I was more soberly accoutred as a medieval magistrate in a black velvet affair that became very hot before the evening was over and the last wassail sipped.

In the midst of a madrigal I came to life. Why not give Alice five Christmas presents, presents that would delight a medieval lady, one to please each of her five senses? By Christmas Eve I had assembled the presents and had them handsomely wrapped and under the tree. For the sense of touch a wimple—what else? (wimples were the fashion again that year). For the sense of taste a plum pudding, baked by a friend from a recipe straight out of the Middle Ages; for the sense of smell, a phial of delicate fragrance; for the sense of hearing a

Gregorian chant authentically performed by the Dominican Sisters of Fichermont.

Last of all, something—but what?—for the sense of sight that would hold in thrall a truly medieval lady. Perhaps a story, but not just any story. It must be one that would gather the sacredness of Christmas with its sacrament of light and leave the heart warmed forever.

St. Luke did this for his friends with his story of the birth of Christ. Doubtless he first heard the report when he visited the shepherds in the Judean hills. (Note Luke 1:65. "The events were talked of through the whole hill country of Judea." See also 2:18.) I did find the perfect story, related by Louis C. Elson in *The National Music of America*. It was the story of a man of the Middle Ages who sang a chorale in the darkness and found that hope was reborn. I copied it off, rolled it up in a handsome scroll tied in a red ribbon, and hung it on the tree.

Christmas Eve on the Niederring

During the fourteenth century the greatest pestilence swept through Europe that has ever been recorded in history. It was called "the Black Death," and claimed its victims by hundreds of thousands, in every country of the old world. In that dreadful epoch men sought to save their lives by isolation. Since a touch, the sweep of a passing garment, might bring death, many barred themselves up in their houses, with such provisions as they could gather, and sustained a strange siege against the invisible enemy without. In such a manner did one of the citizens of Goldberg, in Germany, save his life until a Christmas eve in 1353. He thought himself the last inhabitant of the plague-stricken city, and as the time of the joyous festival approached he could not but recall how many of his old companions had joined with him in merrymaking in the past years; and now he was left alone in the midst of desolaton. The thought must have been borne in upon him that his life was not worth saving at the price of such loneliness, for he unbarred his door and went out into the street to take the plague, if God willed it, and to die. As he went forth he sang the Christmas song that he had sung in the old days with his friends, a "Marien-lied" [a song of Mary], entitled "Uns ist ein Kindlein heut' geborn." He was astounded to hear a voice respond to his own, and in a little while another citizen had unbarred his door and sang with him; as the two went down the street they were joined by another, and another, until, when they had come to the end of the road at the Niederring, a hill close to the town, there was a little band of twenty-five, men, women, and children, all that was left of the town of Goldberg. Whether it was that the plague had spent its violence or, which is more probable, that the minds of the survivors were more serene and less afraid of death, none of this little band died of the Black Death. They returned to their homes, set their houses in order, buried their dead, and the town began to prosper anew. But each Christmas eve for centuries after this event (even to very recent years), the inhabitants of the town gathered together at divine service at midnight, and at two o'clock they marched to the Niederring, where all united in singing the following chorale:

> To us this day is born a child.
> God with us.
> His mother is a virgin mild.
> God with us. God with us,
> Against us who dare be?

A Christmas Shirt for John

"It's really crazy," Alice said, "the way Emily gives John a shirt every Christmas."

"A shirt," I protested mildly, "is not to be sneezed at."

"Ah!" said Alice, "But it's the *same* shirt. Emily and John have everything anybody ever needed for normal living, so Emily thinks it's foolish to clutter up John's den with more things for her to dust. She finally hit on the idea of giving him a shirt for Christmas. When Christmas is over, she hides the shirt for another year, and wraps it up in a fancy new package when Christmas comes around again. John doesn't know the difference, and he's pleased as punch. It wouldn't be Christmas if John didn't find a shirt under the tree. Of course, he doesn't suspect that it's the same shirt she has been giving him for a dozen Christmases. He's so pleased that he always waltzes Emily around the room and tells her she's the best wife a man ever had."

"Isn't that a little like what God is always doing for us at Christmas?" I ventured.

"For instance?" Alice raised a speculative eyebrow, and I could see she surmised I was Drawing Conclusions.

"Well, every December we get gifts we have received the Christmases before, but we couldn't very well do without them. The "Hallelujah Chorus," for instance. It's a gift that would be hard to improve on. If the choir left it out, you'd know for sure something was missing.

"Or the same carols we've heard ever since we were kids. Everyone knows the best ones are the old standbys like "Silent Night," and "The First Noel" and "O Little Town." There haven't been any improvements in carols since the ones we sang dashing through the snow in a one horse open sleigh.

"Or take nativity pageants, God help us! You would spoil Christmas entirely if you left out the shepherds and wise men, the angels and the Holy Family, and, yes, the friendly beasts.

"People could give you more gifts than you could stack in a closet, but none of them would compare with Aunt Betsy's fruitcake or Grandma Sayre's cookies cut out in the shape of Christmas trees—and always the same.

"In other words," I concluded, "for a really scrumptous

Christmas, God is always bringing out the same gifts that he has been giving us for lo these many, and still taking us by surprise again and again, as if we were children waking up for the first time with shining morning faces. Christmas, by all that's holy, is just more and more of the lovely same."

"True!" Alice agreed. "And how would you like a shirt for Christmas?"

"Fine," I said. "Just see that the neck is the right size."

Angel with a Broom

It was late on a Sunday afternoon in Advent. In the undercroft of the church all Bethlehem waited nervously for the signal to make its grand entrance in the nativity play. Plump as a pouter pigeon in her glistening white robes, the Christmas angel shifted her shoulder blades and arched the enormous pair of wings precariously harnessed to them. As angels go she was a knockout.

It was at this juncture that noisy children came streaming out of the settlement house next door to the church. Full of high spirits, they began to let off steam by kicking in two of the basement windows of the church.

At the sound of shattering glass the cast of the nativity play froze—all except the Christmas angel. This remarkably well-organized delegate from the heavenly host laid her hands on a broom and began to sweep up the glass, her white wings tilting in the draft that came through the broken windows.

This, of course, is what Christmas angels always do. You think of them as floating about in the moonlight singing improbabilities about peace on earth, goodwill to men. The truth is that your better type of Christmas angel is more at home with a broom in her hands. She is the one who sweeps up the broken things and tidies up undercrofts—and kitchens.

She is always descending through cloven skies and seeking out shepherds in the cold and frosty night air and sending them off to a stable where the sight of a Child will warm their sluggish blood.

She would want to tell you the Epiphany legend the Italians love about La Befana who refused the invitation to go to Bethlehem the night of the Birth and who takes her old broom and goes sweeping down all the roads of the world.

When a Christmas angel sees a tired mother sweeping her house late at night in search of a lost coin, the way Jesus remembered that Mary did (Luke 15:8), the Christmas angel is likely to be the one to take over the broom.

* * * The Asterisks of Christmas * * *

It was Jennifer, one of the most beguiling of granddaughters, on the phone. "We just finished reading *Romeo and Juliet*," she said with the breathlessness of one who has made a great discovery. "I liked it. It was hard to read because you had to keep looking down at all the footnotes."

Good scholar, Jennifer. And good Christian scholar, Ronald Knox with his appreciation of the scholar's apparatus. He said of the nativity of Christ: "The Star that hangs over the Crib becomes a kind of asterisk, adding footnotes to the plain text." The Gospel *does* begin with a remarkable asterisk, but before it is through with you, you are puzzling over some odd footnotes.

First, you look up and see that dazzling star hovering in the sky. Then you follow down to where its beams point, and you come to a strange little stable full of human hopes and fears.

Next, you lift your head to listen to the heavenly host singing its *Gloria*, but at once you look down the page to a footnote that refers to a very different sort of sound.

Wailing and loud lamentation,
Rachel weeping for her children (Matthew 2:18).

Again, you think you are seeing angels disappear into the glory, but when you consult the footnote it is only a sad little item about Mary and Joseph bundling up their Child and fleeing in the night.

Always we keep looking up at the star, and always it refers us to some obscure footnote that, left to ourselves, we would have missed. Though we find it hard to comprehend the mystery beyond mystery from which the light has come, at least the footnotes to which it points are legible—the No Vacancy sign on the inn door, the assassination of the children, the disappearance of displaced persons into alien lands.

It is hard to see how anyone could ever have made religion out of the footnotes, but this is precisely what people did. Because they had known what it was like to be poor or rejected, they found it easy to identify with the people in the footnotes.

It was harder to see what relation the footnotes had to that asterisk up there in the sky. But they listened to Rachel weeping for her children until they were sure they could hear another sound coming out of timelessness into time.

These asterisks and their footnotes follow consistently throughout the ministry of Jesus. Begin with his baptism when he sees the heavens opened and hears the confirmation that he is the beloved Son; but the asterisk refers to a footnote that relates how he is presently surrounded by wild beasts in a less than human landscape.

Or recall the Mount of Transfiguration when Jesus seemed

to his disciples to disappear into light. But the footnote to this is an epileptic boy whom no one has been able to heal.

We sing about the cross of our Lord "towering o'er the wrecks of time," but the cross too is another asterisk in the term paper of history. We look down the page to the footnotes where faith must sometimes walk in the dark and where love has little to offer but its own brokenness.

"The star of Bethlehem," said Paul Scherer, "was like an asterisk in the text of history; and this was a footnote at the bottom of the page: Whoever wants to be great among you must be your servant" (Matthew 20:26).

How does the soul find its vocation? Or what gives to some the urgency to preach Christ? I have had occasion to ask a number of candidates for the ministry what led them to their decision. Some of them reported an experience when faith like a great lamp shone in their hearts. Others found that their call had come through the summons of human need. For some it was faith's asterisk, for others the footnote of shadowed thresholds that set their feet in the Way.

For my own part, if I could wish my friends true Christmas, it would be in the words of one whose name is long forgotten but whose Christmas promise burns like faith's asterisk in the night sky.

Whosoever on ye nighte of ye nativity of ye young Lord Jesus, in ye great snows, shall fare forth bearing a succulent bone for ye loste and lamenting hounde, a wisp of hay for ye shivering horse, a cloak of warm raiment for ye stranded wayfarer, a flagon of red wine for him whose marrow withers, a garland of bright berries for one who has worn chains, gay arias of lute and harp for all huddled birds who thought that song was dead, and divers lush sweetmeats for such babes' faces as peer from lonely windows—

To him shall be proffered and returned gifts of such an astonishment as will rival hues of ye peacock and the harmonies of heaven, so that though he live to ye greate age when man goes stooping and querulous because of ye nothing that is left in him, yet shall he walk upright and remembering, as one whose heart shines like a great star in his breaste.

The Twelve Little Christmas Trees

I feel sorry for a Christmas tree, and then I buy it—the kind that splays out in three lonely branches at the top. It's the effect of being reared on "The Little Fir Tree."

—Ann Webb

"Remarkable!" Alice said. "I don't know why I didn't think of it before."

"Yes?" I said with only mild apprehension in my tone.

"We ought to do something to gussie up the patio for Christmas," Alice said. "What would you think of setting out twelve small Christmas trees around it?"

"Small Christmas trees," I said doubtfully, "grow into big Christmas trees."

"There was that little fir tree of Hans Christian Andersen's," Alice said. "It never grew to be a very big fir tree."

"That's because someone cut it down," I said. "Given half a chance, it would have spread out amazingly. Oliver Wendell Holmes used to have certain elms he called his tree wives. He would throw his arms around them."

"I wouldn't go for a forest of tree wives just outside our window," Alice said. "I am all the wife you need."

"How many Christmas trees do you think it would take?" I asked, beginning to weaken.

We set off for a tree nursery and fell in love with every small Christmas tree on the plantation. Before we knew it, we had purchased twelve irresistible trees. They were delivered on a bright, brisk morning early in December, and I began to plant them while Alice held them up straight.

"We ought to name our twelve trees," Alice said.

"Maybe we could name them after the twelve apostles," I suggested.

"One of them went bad," Alice said. "We wouldn't want that to happen to one of our beautiful Christmas trees."

"Maybe we could name them after the twelve lords a-leaping in the old carol," I proposed.

"Or the twelve bright shiners," Alice countered.

"Who are the twelve bright shiners?" I asked.

"They're in 'Greensleeves,'" Alice said. "I have it! The twelve bright shiners are our grandchildren. We'll name the trees after them and have twelve grandchildren Christmas trees. As the grandchildren grow, so will the trees, and each child will have a tree that is especially his. Melissa Christmas tree. Derek and Don and Heather and Hillary Christmas trees—"

"You've hit it," I said.

"There is just one problem, suppose we had a thirteenth grandchild?"

In the end we rushed back to the nursery and purchased the most beautiful little Christmas tree of all. We set out our thirteenth Christmas tree under a downspout so that if ever we need it in a hurry it will be flourishing. Like Christmas, a grandchild is living proof you have started something you can't finish.

$100,000 for Christmas

It was a sad night, all right. An arsonist had set the beautiful old church on fire. When I arrived at midnight, the flames softly licking through the roof sounded like ten thousand cats licking up cream. A long series of autumn Sundays followed when we worshiped in the gymnasium of a school. But it wasn't the same—except for the cross and candlesticks that had followed us there. The truth was that the odor of old gym shoes hung heavy on the air. We wondered if would carry this aroma with us into the new church we were going to build.

Then, just a week before Christmas a check for $100,000 arrived from the insurance company. It was my duty to see it safely deposited in a bank downtown.

I set off blithely enough, but as I threaded my way through the throngs of Christmas shoppers I could see that something sinister was beginning to happen to me.

The shoppers all seemed to be happy people in search of just the right present for their best beloved. Some of them were whistling, and most had made a party of it and were exchanging pleasantries with their friends as they stode rapidly along in the frosty air. But the $100,000 in my pocket put a different cast on everything and everyone. It occurred to me that it would be just my luck to be robbed, and at this, the very street turned menacing. I began rapidly to lose my faith in Christmas throngs in gay apparel. Suppose that an unsuspected hand were even now reaching into my pocket and making off with the majestic check. It was a thought to make the blood run cold. I kept casting a wary eye over my shoulder to see if someone might be slipping up behind me. Frankly, I did not trust these people. They might look innocent enough, but surely one of them was even then plotting to undo me.

To my astonishment, no one gave me so much as the time of

day. Here I was with a check for $100,000, and no one so much as brushed up against me with larcenous intentions.

I admit I began to feel a little disappointed. The least one has a right to expect when he has such a huge sum in his pocket is first degree murder. I arrived a little ruefully at the bank and found an interminable line of people cashing Christmas checks ahead of me. "Come down to queue in lilac time," I told myself stoically and inched my way to the teller.

"At least," I thought, "the teller will be impressed when he sees a check for $100,000."

The teller wasn't. Not the slightest shock of recognition crossed his weary face. He canceled the check, looked up, and called out, "Next!"

"What," I asked myself, "is the world coming to when you can carry around assets like this and no one so much as gives you a tumble?"

Then—but it took some time for this to happen—it occurred to me that if the paltry $100,000 in my pocket could turn my trusting heart to deep suspicion of the innocent Christmas shoppers all around me, no wonder Jesus had said that "it will be hard for a rich man to enter the kingdom of heaven" (Matthew 19:23). Your rich man would be so infernally obsessed to protect his small freehold that he would never see the poor asking for a crust of bread. When you are in that shape, you have missed the kingdom of God.

I came to a sudden halt and made a petition to the Most High. "O Lord," I prayed, "don't ever let me become rich!"

And the Lord who answers prayer has taken care of that ever since.

Christmas, the Great Amateur Open

In a world of professional sports, of professional politicians, and of Lords High Everything Else there are still people like me who sing the praises of the amateur. This Advent I salute the non-professional.

When you come to think of it, this is what God is doing all the time. He is a God who singles out amateurs for his most important assignments. Take the year when Augustus was emperor in Rome and Quirinius was governor of Syria—experts both in their line. Just the ones for the Word of the Lord to come to. But no, that was the year that an unknown maid learned that hers was to be a destiny greater than theirs.

Or take the shepherds, big rough fellows from the hills, not the sort to be invited to a great nativity. A life in the frosty air beating wolves away from the flock wasn't guaranteed to turn a shepherd into a very special guest. But now they are rushing into town thinking, "Whatever it is that is happening, amateurs like us are welcome!"

Or take the wise men. Your professional wise man would only have followed a dependable star, not the queer one that went blinking out the moment he reached Jerusalem. Someone should have told these bearded old men with eyes like coals burning in their gaunt faces, "Wise men, you are rank amateurs. You seek a child, and all you can think of for presents are gold, frankincense, and myrrh. This goes to show how little you know about a baby who needs a warm blanket and plenty of swaddling clothes."

The drowsy old men would have nodded their heads sagely and agreed. "How stupid of us not to have thought of it! But Christmas is the great amateur open, and you don't have to be a very smart wise man to get an invitation. After all, we *have* found the Child, and maybe the gold and frankincense and myrrh will help a little in the hidden years ahead."

And the quiet of the land—nobody very special here—people to whom it would never have occurred to call Joseph and Mary the Holy Family, people who maybe didn't arrive in time for the wonderful birth, but who always seemed to be on call when needed. Cousin Elizabeth and her husband Zechariah of whom you wouldn't be likely to hear again, but who had had an intimation so intense that he was tongue-tied for months afterward.

Or take Anna and Simeon, who are themselves shadows haunting the deeper shadows of the temple, peering into the face of each new child who comes their way, hoping to be the first to lay their tired old eyes on the sleeping face of the Child of the promise.

What amateurs all of them are! No style. No class. But now they have overheard our criticism and are unembarrassed in concurring. "You've hit us off to a *T*," they say. "We're none of us professional. You know our names only because we were stupid enough to blunder into the Bible. We're just the sort of folks who live down your street, none of us distinguished. The only reason you know us is that Christmas is the great amateur open, so we dared to come."

I suppose this is why we find our way back to Bethlehem every year at Christmas time. See, just ahead is the house of Joseph the carpenter, and yes, that is Mary with her broom sweeping up a shaving as you enter her door. At once you know that you are among amateurs. You will never again have to pretend that you are something you are not. It suddenly strikes you that if you become as a little child and exult uninhibitedly in all things beautiful, you too can experience the uncomplicated joy of being an amateur—with great expectations.

Angels Rush In

The elves are elbowing the angels about for a special place on the mantle.
—from a Christmas letter

Those pushy elves! Assigned to maximum visibility in our Christmas festivities, and what do they do? Shove the very angels off the mantle and send them crashing. So typical of how we treat the hosts of heaven today, dismissing them out of hand, along with that world of personal being that once fostered all that was lyric in the heart. Throwing the baby out with the bath.

We are apt to treat as odd joseys people of old who like St. Louis of France professed to have daily converse with angels. We scarcely know what to make of Joan of Arc with her testimony that angels from on high visited her—"The angels? Why, they often come among us. Others may not see them, but I do." Or what shall we make of poets like William Blake who insisted he saw angels in his garden? People in our time seem little given to visions, or, if they have them, hesitate to speak of them lest they be thought a little strange. It was otherwise on the lonely farms in the valley where I grew up and where I was first a minister. People were more solitary then, more at home with stillness and the fields and the sky. People often spoke to me of that personal world the Bible had taught them to know, a world where good and evil were personal embodiments.

I recall one old woman remembering the day when her little child died. She had thought herself alone in the room with her dead child, when through a mist of tears she saw the white-winged hosts of heaven descend on either side of the cradle where the little one lay, saw them lift the child ever so gently before they laid her back on a pillow. Her faith in the love of God had bodied itself forth as a vision of angels that she had seen through the lens of her tears. Faith gives us "new eyes for invisibles" as Rufus Jones said. Francis Thompson put it even better.

> The angels keep their ancient places,
> Turn but a stone, and start a wing!

The Reverend Louis Tucker, who was rector of a parish in Louisiana, had an experience of this order. In a culture where men seldom attended worship, he felt a sickness in his heart at the failure of his ministry to appeal to the men of the community. The choir, all women, their voices thin and untrained, was a painful experience to his sensitive ear. The half-empty church defeated him. Then one afternoon at evensong he saw them, the hosts of heaven, breaking through into the dimness of the choir, standing there unobserved by the congregation, rank on rank; heard their voices, the rumble of baritones, the fluting exaltation of the tenors, a choir invisible to all eyes but his own, supplementing the poor human offering of praise, heard them, saw them, in wondering awe. Though he was never to see them again, he knew they were always there, invisible but real, ready to rush in where fools would never think of treading.

> In old days there were angels who came and took men by the hand and led them away from the city of destruction. We see no white-winged angels now. But yet men are led away from threatening destruction: a hand is put into theirs, which leads them forth gently towards a calm and bright land, so that they look no more backward; and the hand may be a little child's.

Storyteller's Christmas Bag

(The words capitalized in this story are articles you will want to tuck into an old pillowcase before you appear with it slung over your shoulder. Pull out of your bag these properties as you come to them in telling the story.)

The proper way to tell a Christmas story, I submit, is first to pack your storyteller's bag full of presents for the Christ Child, then sling the bag over your shoulder and come to the party. How your story will begin, of course, will depend on what comes to hand when you pull your presents out of the bag. But I am never surprised when I reach in and find my hand connecting with a STAR.

This is the way the great storytellers who started telling the story a thousand years before Jesus was born begin their tale, because a star is the first thing that comes to hand. Ten centuries before Jesus was born there was a wise man from the East who sang a song about a very special star that "would come forth out of Jacob" (Numbers 24:17). This old wise man was a poet who knew in his heart that someone beautiful would some day be born in Israel, and his story of the star no one ever forgot.

Since the heart has its reasons, a Christmas star does not have to compete with all the other stars in their heavenly orbits. It can rise out of a race of holy people who are called of God according to his purpose.

Of course, there is no point in having a star like this without having three wise men to follow it. When Jacobus de Voragine wrote *The Golden Legend* seven hundred years ago, he put the three wise men in *his* story bag and gave them high-sounding Latin names—Melchior, which means "king of light," Gaspar, which means "the white one"—I see him as an ancient king with a beautiful white beard—and Balthazar, which means "lord of treasures."

I always mount Melchior, Gaspar and Balthazar on sturdy camels and send them swinging across the shifting sand of great and terrible deserts. If you listen hard, you can begin to hear their CAMEL BELLS now as they swing along in the cool night wind following their star. And yes, I just happen to have in my storyteller's bag the very camel bells you thought you were hearing. "A cold coming" they had of it, but it is always a big help on a long journey if someone is ringing a bell.

If it seems hard to imagine the deserts they are crossing to be with us at the birth of the little Child who is going to be King of our lives, let me reach into my bag to see if I can find a DESERT, and—yes, this is the very thing, or at least a tiny part of it. This sand a friend of mine brought me from a desert near Caesarea Phillipi that Jesus used to visit. It isn't beyond the power of imagination to think that Jesus might once have left his footprint on this very sand that I am pouring from a phial. You would feel a kind of awe if you were walking softly down the aisle to the altar of your church, feeling sure you were walking in the footprints of Jesus. Well, so you are!

All roads lead to Bethlehem if you want them to. And now our three wise men, King of Light, the White One, and Lord of Treasures, are riding down the Street of the Star, and past the well that will one day be named the Well of the Virgin and from which you may drink if you go there.

They find the overcrowded inn. They are shown to the manger where that beautiful mother is and her Child and Joseph leaning on his staff. The wise ones fall on their knees because they have found the place, and they have found the Child. Jacobus tells us that "among the ancients it was the custom never to present oneself before a god or king without offering gifts; and the Wise Men, who came from the country of Persia and Chaldea . . . brought the gifts which the Persians and the Chaldeans were wont to offer." GOLD, and I just happen to have brought you some. Although it looks like a heap of golden coins, it is really chocolates wrapped in gold foil with a piece for each of you. That is the gift that the Lord of Treasures brought the Christ Child.

When I reach into my storyteller's bag, what do I find now but some genuine FRANKINCENSE and MYRRH that have come from the places where the wise men found them first. Later, maybe you will want to touch the frankincense and myrrh. If you do, remember that these were the strange, beautiful presents that Melchior and Balthazar brought, and that the Virgin Mary cupped her hands around such fragrances as these. If I were to set them alight, you would detect an incense like that which hovered in the air around the sacrifices commanded of ancient Israel. Jacobus again, "The royalty, the divinity, and the humanity of Christ"—these are what the gifts of the wise men signify, "because gold is used for royal tribute and He was the highest King, incense for divine worship, since He was God, and myrrh for the burial of the dead, since He was a mortal man."

Of course, if the only ones who came to the manger were the wise men, not many people would ever have started for Bethlehem, because wise men are an endangered species. Sometimes you go for a whole year and do not meet even one. But there are always poor folks in the world, millions of us, and we came too, bending our heads low to come in out of the frosty air into the manger.

And what luck! For we are just in time to see the shepherds on their way down from the shepherds' field above Bethlehem. The story they have to tell is like a dream, full of angels they have seen, and of *Glorias* so thrilling that only our choirs can match them.

The shepherds ran all the way to Bethlehem, and this would not be easy, because there are sharp stones in the field, and yes, inside my storyteller's bag is a sharp little piece of chert that actually came from the shepherds' field above Bethlehem, and one of our shepherds may have pricked his foot on it as he ran long ago.

But on that particular night I think he would not have noticed because if you ever once in your life knelt before the Holy Family, you would forget all about yourself in the awe you would feel, especially when you found yourself kneeling next to a wise man.

It would be only when they looked up that the shepherds would feel a little foolish because the wise men had brought such stunning gifts—the gold and frankincense and myrrh. And they, the shepherds, the poor of the earth, had failed to bring anything at all.

But yes, one of the shepherds is reaching into my storyteller's Christmas bag, for he knows I would never want poor folk to be embarrassed when they have nothing to give. And see, he has found a LAMB, which is exactly the thing that this child, who will one day be called the Lamb of God, will want more than anything else.

Of course, if I had a Christmas story bag big enough to hold all the presents we should like to bring to him, it would have to be as big as the world. No one storyteller would be strong enough to tote it. But really, the kind of gifts this Child would like the best are gifts that do not weigh anything at all—carols that are the heart's own joyous music and that you can see going straight up to heaven with your frosty breath on a cold winter's night, forgiveness that tosses a mantle of mercy over all the old world's ancient wrongs, and prayers that climb the altar stairs to God. These are the greater gifts, greater than shepherd or wise man ever brought, and ours to bring each hour of every day for all the years to be.

In a moment we shall sing another carol, then bow our heads to receive the blessing, and go joyously out to find where our Street of the Star begins. As you go, may the season hold its choicest gifts in store for you, gifts of love and goodwill.

On Shifting Gears for Advent

Purple is also the color of sorrow and penitence. It is the liturgical color for Advent and Lent, the Church's seasons of preparation and penitence, when men are anticipating the joyous festivals of Christmas and Easter.

—George Ferguson: *Signs and Symbols in Christian Art*

One of the things that gives me a bad time is trying to shift gears spiritually when the Christian calendar inaugurates a new season. I admit I don't automatically feel the way the calendar insists I am supposed to feel. Sometimes my mood actually contradicts all the expectations of that worthy ordering of the Christian year.

For instance, Advent goes purple with penitence, a season when your true Christian ought to go in for sweetly solemn thoughts and fastings and humorless self-denials. But very often that is not the way that Advent affects me. Just when I have finished reading a brace of penitential psalms or maybe the book of Lamentations and think I am getting into the proper spirit, I wake up some bright December morning about a week into Advent as happy as a lark and feeling like a stroll downtown.

Almost everybody I run into on the street appears to feel the same way too. People smile happily. Strangers nod a greeting. The whole world looks rosy at the moment, and you see no cheeks stained with penitential tears. A downright good feeling wells up in laughter, which only increases your certainty that if not all is right with the world, at least Main Street is still in business.

Do you know what I think? I think God may approve of the ecclesiastical calendar on general principles, but if a man marries a pretty wife and finds out that she is also a good cook—a bonus he knows he doesn't deserve—God would not want that man, Advent or no Advent, to get stuffy about his religion. Right in the middle of Advent I'll bet that God would say to that man, "I'm the One who loves a cheerful heart you read about in the Book."

In the last century the Church of England had a Dr. Pusey who appointed himself an apostle of gloom. He was the brother who led his church in a campaign to bring back holiness and other-worldliness. I guess he did it, but he had a dreadful idea of the holy. He vowed that for years no one would ever see him smile. And no one did. I wonder if during that awful time he ever stole away to another town where nobody knew him and walked down Main Street, his mouth stretched in a big smile from ear to ear.

When Advent comes, some bright morning when you can't remember anything you ought to feel penitent about, go ahead—walk down Main Street feeling as happy as an Ohio cornfield when all the stalks are tasseling out.

On the other hand, remember that Carl Sandburg used to say, "Be happy, kid, be happy, but not too doubled-up doggone happy."

Our Christmas Rows

It was one of those December evenings when the world is being blanketed with snow, a wind out of the north country is whistling with the help of a loose shingle, and Christmas is just around the corner—the sort of night to find a friendly fire and settle down beside it with a pan of popcorn on your knees while your wife is on the opposite side of the hearth catching up on her reading.

"Just the moment," I proposed, "to conclude that if there are any traces of original sin left around, they will promptly wither and die."

"Hardly!" Alice rejoined, turning a page of the *New York Times Book Review*. "Just listen to the English playwright John Osborne remembering his family. 'Disappointment was oxygen to them,' he writes of the bitter, quarreling family whose Christmas rows were the only action in their fixed lives. 'The grudge that was their birthright they pursued with passionate despondency to the grave.'"

"Their *Christmas* rows?" I inquired.

"People have them," Alice insisted. "I used to know a family that specialized in them. No sooner had the turkey come steaming on the dinner table than the mother of this family launched her annual Christmas row. She would dredge up some embarrassment that everybody else had all but forgotten—usually about her husband's Aunt Agatha's tendency to forget and leave her teeth at home when she came on a visit—and indulge in a period of spitefulness.

"By the time her family was well into the plum pudding, everything was at sixes and sevens, with the guests all taking sides. If one side faltered during this Christmas row, the mother would nip in on the losing side and stoke the fire again. By the time dinner was over everybody hated everybody else."

"Jean-Paul Sartre," I put in mildly, "used to say that 'Hell is other people.'"

"It *was* at the Christmas rows in *that* family," Alice said.

"You and I don't seem to have many Christmas rows," I observed. "Do you think we are missing out on a good thing?"

"I guess not," Alice said. "But come to think of it, didn't Christmas begin with a row? There was horrid old King Herod breathing forth threatenings and slaughtering the innocents."

"That," I said, "is the reason for Christmas. It is the ultimate Great Surprise. It can come not only to firesides like ours with our 'wee bit ingle blinkin' bonnily,' as Robert Burns put it, but

91

to cold prisons where the likes of Martin Niemoeller are only a hand's breadth away from death, and a Christmas row is brewing for fair."

Above the raving of the winter wind we began to hear the piping voices of children caroling at our door.

> And the star rains its fire
> While the beautiful sing,
> For the manger of Bethlehem
> Cradles a King!

"You couldn't have a Christmas row when anything as heavenly as that is happening," Alice said.

"Come Christmas," I promised, "you'll find two stockings hung by the chimney with care."

The Women of Christmas

This is the season the young heart sings
Of truant shepherds and star-mazed kings;
But best of all—though you think me daft—
Is the rippling laughter Sarah laughed
When she was crowding ninety-one
To learn she would birth an impossible son.

And this is the season of new life,
As who should know but Manoah's wife.
An angel who wouldn't tell his name
Went soaring up in a searing flame,

But first he promised her the joy
That she'd hold in her aching arms a boy.

And what shall I say of that little town
Where a virgin stared an angel down
And learned of all impossible things
That she would mother the King of kings?

Then let the bells in the steeple chime
For Elizabeth who was past her prime
To suckle a child, yet a child's lips pressed
Against the curve of her aging breast.

These are four whose wombs were stirred
By the whisper of God's unfailing Word.
So tune your flutes and sound your drum,
For barren woman, your time will come.

And prithee, what shall I say more
Of the wife of star-led Melchior,
A shining woman of patient thrift
Whose dowry purchased a royal gift?

Or what of Gaspar's dutiful spouse
Who stayed at home and kept his house?
And what of the wife of Balthasár
Who was the first to see the star?

These are three who prayed all day
For their men to return another way,
Each of whom bore a beautiful child
In deserts where the winds were wild.

So, strolling players, one and all,
Who feast within our Christmas hall,

And shepherds, late from field and byre,
Who come to share our Christmas fire;
And lordlings all, with your myths of power:
The women of Christmas will have their hour.

Then troll a carol, troubadours,
For a greening earth will soon be yours;
And hearken well to this my lay:
The women of Christmas will have their day,
The women of Christmas will have their day.

—Based on Genesis 18:12, Judges 13, St. Luke 1

Whispers of Divinity

Whispers of divinity—it is these that guide us truly to the mother of our Lord. The Virgin Mary may not fit into everybody's theology—but she fits into everybody's heart. So it is natural for St. Luke to ponder the lore of the Holy Maid who went a far journey to bear her little Son, and for St. Matthew to gather in his breast all the starlight he could accumulate.

In their turn the greatest artists have sought to portray the one who held the Christ Child against her breast. A maid who did that is bound to be dear to us all.

This power of the Maid to reach out her arms, not only to her own child, but to all our waiting hearts, is undiminished. On the holy island of Iona rising out of the mists is a sculpture of the Virgin that bears this legend:

Jacob Lipschitz, faithful to the Jewish
faith of his ancestors, had made this
Virgin for the sake of goodwill among
men on earth, so that the spirit may reign.

Good old St. Matthew! And good old St. Luke! And good old Jacob Lipschitz!—all of them creating an imagery the heart understands best at Christmas.

The day would come when the Virgin Mary would be celebrated as the Queen of Heaven, but she comes closer to many of us in the prophecy of Simeon that a sword would pierce though her soul (Luke 2:35). If we love Christ at all, a sword pierces our own souls also whenever we draw near to his cross.

G. K. Chesterton relates a poignant memory of his visit to Poland. There he had made the acquaintance of a young Count

whose huge and costly palace of a country house . . . had been . . . left in ruins by the retreat of the Red Army after the Battle of Warsaw. Looking at such a mountain of shattered marbles and black and blasted tapestries, one of our party said, "It must be a terrible thing for you to see your old family home destroyed like this." But the young man . . . shrugged his shoulders . . . "Oh, I do not blame them for that," he said . . . . "There is only one thing I really resent. I will show it to you."

And he led us out into a long avenue lined with poplars; and at the end of it was a statue of the Blessed Virgin; with the head and the hands shot off. But the hands had been lifted; and it is a strange thing that the very mutilation seemed to give more meaning to the attitude of intercession; asking mercy for the merciless race of men.

So Christmas comes, sometimes out of havoc and betrayal, the heart quite numb with pain, comes with a crèche for remembrance and a Virgin and a Holy Child and friendly beasts to help us find our way back through time to the high places of the singing spirit of our living God.